Civil Rights Warrior

Civil Rights Warrior

A Life on the Front Lines of Justice, Equality, and the American Dream

EVELYN JONES RICH

Skyhorse Publishing

Skyhorse Publishing books may be purchased in bulk at special discounts for sales promotion, corporate gifts, fund-raising, or educational purposes. Special editions can also be created to specifications. For details, contact the Special Sales Department, Skyhorse Publishing, 307 Fifth Avenue, 4th Floor, New York, NY 10016 or info@skyhorsepublishing.com.

10 9 8 7 6 5 4 3 2 1

Library of Congress Cataloging-in-Publication Data is available on file.

Cover design by David Ter-Avanesyan
Cover images courtesy of the auhtor

Print ISBN: 978-1-5107-8565-6
Ebook ISBN: 978-1-5107-8566-3

Printed in the United States of America

To Mother, Marvin, MaryAnn,
and all the girls and women allies
in our continuing struggle for social justice.
Never give up!

Contents

1

Debating Malcolm X

My husband, Marvin, called to tell me that I must debate Malcolm X the very next day. To be specific, Malcolm X wanted to debate a representative of the Congress of Racial Equality (CORE) about the Freedom Rides. It was May 1961. Ku Klux Klan members and others had just burned a bus carrying CORE Freedom Riders in Anniston, Alabama. The entire nation was aware of what was happening because photos of the burning bus were plastered on the front pages of newspapers across the country.

Malcolm X hoped to capitalize on this awful event by presenting the Nation of Islam's (a.k.a. Black Muslims) viewpoint, which insisted upon meeting violence with violence—a rejection of CORE's nonviolent response mandate. As spokesperson for the Nation of Islam and leader of their New York City chapter, he was a significant figure in the civil rights movement.

The riders left Washington, DC, days earlier on their way to New Orleans as part of the 2nd Freedom Rides. The initial "Rides"—the Journey of Reconciliation—occurred in 1947, targeting the upper Southern states in response to the Supreme Court's 1947 Irene Morgan Decision outlawing discrimination in Interstate Commerce. *Morgan vs. VA*—328 U.S.373 (1946)—is a famous civil rights case. Irene Morgan was arrested in Virginia for refusing to give up her seat on a bus. She sued, and the Supreme Court ruled that states cannot discriminate against passengers in interstate commerce by requiring that they sit in certain parts of the bus. Morgan was on her way to another state.

The decisive clause is found in Article I, Clause 5, Section 8. The (Edward) Boynton Supreme Court decision—346 U.S. 451 (1960)—reinforced the Morgan decision, declaring that states could not discriminate in interstate travel, including restaurants, bathrooms, and other facilities associated with travel.

Marvin—I often called him "Marvie"—was CORE's Community Relations Director. Among many duties, he led CORE's public relations efforts. The problem, Marvie told me, was that Jim Farmer, CORE's national director and primary leader, was in jail as part of CORE's "jail not bail" response to the resistance the sit-ins generated. Jail not bail was yet another CORE initiative fighting prejudice and discrimination enveloping the nation. Funds for bail were scarce as the number of students sitting-in at lunch counters across the country increased.

"I can't send a White person," he said. "You'll be perfect. Just don't let him intimidate you. The debate is tomorrow."

"I must arrange for Gordon's care," I responded. Our son was three years old, and television was in its infancy in 1961. I often had difficulty finding babysitters when I wanted to attend an evening CORE meeting with Marvin because we didn't have a television set. Young people who lived in our co-op refused to babysit because we couldn't provide a source of entertainment. We also took Gordon with us on picket lines when we couldn't afford a babysitter. Irma Horowitz, my neighbor and close friend at Queensview West where we lived, agreed that Gordon could spend the next day with her daughter. Marvin would pick him up from Irma and put him to bed the following evening.

Marvin and I had no money because he worked for CORE for about $10,000 a year. We lived in a lower-middle-income cooperative apartment development in New York City. My job was to care for our son, to help him become a productive citizen when he grew up. I felt that it was imperative to instill self-confidence and a sense of self that would serve as valuable weapons when Gordon confronted future challenges as a "Negro" male.

Ultimately, I went to Philadelphia by bus because it was cheaper than the train. I'm from Philadelphia, where the debate was held. My family lived in Wissahickon, an integrated, working-class section of Philadelphia not far from WCAU, the radio station hosting the debate. I took the bus to my mother's house, explained why I was there, and then took another bus to City Line Avenue where WCAU was located.

I remember Marvin's warning, "Evie, don't let Malcolm X intimidate you." I replied, "Don't worry; I'm not afraid of Malcolm X." I'd heard him speak on street corners in New York City—specifically on 125th Street in Harlem, where he spoke regularly. When we picketed Woolworth's on 125th Street on Saturdays, I listened to him. Alex Haley had not yet collaborated with Malcolm X in producing *The Autobiography of Malcolm X as Told to Alex Haley*, one of the great books of our time. By the time the book was published in 1964, Malcolm X had changed many of his basic views.

CORE would normally send James (Jim) Farmer because he was a wonderful speaker. But Farmer, jailed previously, was again incarcerated at forty-one years of age. Decades earlier, Farmer was active in the Wiley College Debate Club when Wiley challenged the Harvard Debate team in the 1935 National Championships. Against predicted odds, the Wiley team won, suggesting the rigor of their preparation and magnificent delivery. *The Great Debaters*, a 2007 film directed by Denzel Washington, captures the drama surrounding the event. Farmer's debate experience served him well. A founder of the Congress of Racial Equality (CORE) in 1942, he helped transform it into one of the most effective civil rights organizations by the 1960s.

Marvie was emphatic. "You must do it because we can't send Farmer, and our other Black leaders are all in jail or in a hospital." I was twenty-eight; Malcolm X was thirty-six. To tell the truth, I didn't need much preparation. As a regional representative, I was a major spokesperson for CORE's operation in the Northeast. Steeped in CORE's philosophy, I was extremely active in New York. Jimmy Robinson, our second in command along with Marvin, was available, but Marvin passed over him because Jimmy was White.

I agreed to go because he had no one else to send. Indeed, I was a very good choice. I had debate experience as president of our high school debate club. I spoke at conferences and conventions while active in student government at Bryn Mawr College. In 1956, I represented the United States at a NATO Youth Conference in Paris. I was a member of the US Delegation to a World Assembly of Youth (WAY) Conference later in Berlin—also in 1956—and chaired the US Delegation to the World Assembly of Youth Conference in Delhi, India, in 1958. The Cold War was at its height. WAY brought together young people from across the globe. Our group, the Young Adult Council (YAC), represented youth from the non-communist world.

I regularly accompanied James Baldwin—we called him Jimmy—the famous African American writer and civil rights activist, on speeches to raise funds for CORE sit-ins. Targeting wealthy Long Island towns, we raised quite a bit of money. Jimmy Baldwin gave the presentation, and I made the pitch—asking audience members to open their wallets and give generously. Wherever Marvie said, "Evie, you have to go," I went.

By 1961, Malcolm X was the Minister of Temple No.12 in Harlem after leading Temples in Detroit, Boston, and Philadelphia. As both the regional representative and chairman of CORE's NYC's Employment Committee, I was involved in a host of activities, including negotiations with targeted employers.

Malcolm X was tall, good-looking, and charismatic. His petty crimes began at age nine and continued into his late teens. Introduced to the principles of Islam while spending six years in prison for burglary and larceny, he was paroled in 1952. Malcolm X quickly became influential in the activist Black Muslim community. Alex Haley's astonishing *Autobiography of Malcolm X* describes how he used his prison time to his advantage—reading widely, including the dictionary. A gifted speaker despite being a high school dropout, he used his rhetorical skills to promote the basic philosophy of Black Muslims, which embraced self-esteem, Black empowerment, and the creation of a new Black state in Africa.

His message was new, uplifting, and challenging—particularly for "Negro" men and women, but especially for young Blacks drawn to his ministry. Malcolm X insisted that Black people have no voice in this country. In his view, the rhetoric of the Constitution and Declaration of Independence was meaningless. Freedom, justice, and equality were beyond our reach. The government was both unable and unwilling to protect us.

Malcolm X was most effective in describing the litany of ills Black people in the United States faced decades after slavery ended, along with the burdens of its aftermath. He cited Jim Crow laws, poll taxes, lynchings, poor schools, limited educational opportunities, residential segregation, discrimination in employment, and poor health care. He provided graphic details illustrating how Black men and women in America would remain second-class citizens long after his death. He rejected nonviolence, CORE's hallmark, and insisted that people of color defend themselves when attacked "by any means necessary."

CORE was first organized and founded in March 1942 in Chicago, Illinois, by a diverse group of integrated graduate students and other activists committed to civil rights. James Farmer was the first national director. CORE accepted Mahatma Gandhi's principles of nonviolent direct action. Acknowledging society's shortcomings, CORE insisted that change was possible. Racial justice can be achieved through nonviolent means. Everyone loses in the face of continuing practices that belittle and deny equal opportunity to Negroes.

The radio program broadcasting the debate, titled *The Talk of Philadelphia*, was hosted by veteran reporter Ed Harvey, a pioneer of Philadelphia talk show programs. Harvey told the Broadcast Pioneers that he was the first person in the Delaware Valley to put callers on the phone. During the show, guests debated among themselves for the first half hour or so, followed by a call-in portion where people raised questions with the debaters or made comments.

For this debate, Malcolm X, Eustace Gay—treasurer and general manager of the *Philadelphia Tribune*, the oldest continuously published African American newspaper in the United States—and I were the guests. Despite the passing years, I remember quite a bit about the debate. We each made opening statements. Like Malcolm X, I was (and remain) a very good speaker without notes. Malcolm X started by making statements and asking me questions. I responded to his questions and asked him questions. When he took a position, I didn't wait for him to finish but jumped right in. Mr. Gay, the third guest, had little to say because neither Malcolm X nor I gave him an opportunity. It wasn't a very orderly debate. Every time Malcolm X made a point that I disagreed with, I interrupted him and said, "I don't agree with you." Then I told him why.

For example, he insisted, "The Bible says money is the root of all evil." I immediately countered, "Malcolm, the Bible doesn't say that. The Bible says in Timothy I:6:10 that the *love* of money is the root of all evil." That really stopped him in his tracks. I went to Sunday School for many, many years and knew the Bible quite well. When he quoted additional Bible verses, I retorted, "Now, wait a minute. That's not what is written in the Bible; this is what it says." I could cite the chapter and verse he was referring to, which really surprised him.

We went back and forth. Of course, Malcolm attacked the basic principles of CORE, including: Love your neighbor. When someone does something you disagree with, discuss it with them, as a neighbor. I would use the word "confront," but CORE would never employ that word. Marvin was committed to CORE and to the principles of nonviolent direct action. I wasn't at the very beginning and said, "Look, this is not how I was brought up; if someone hits me, I'm going to hit them back!" Marvin replied, "Well, you can't do that. You have to turn the other cheek." I answered, "Marvin, where are you coming from? That doesn't make any sense."

By 1961, we had been married for almost five years. Over those years, I watched him repeatedly implement nonviolent direct-action principles. I must admit, grudgingly, that I saw them work. I was shocked, because I was highly skeptical. Marvie insisted on living his life according to these principles. Determined to convince me that I should live my life that way, he finally converted me, but it did not come easily.

In any event, Malcolm X made comments about the White "devil," how terrible he was, and how we would always be oppressed as Black people. "Negroes" was his term. I argued, "Well, I agree with you about the oppression, but I also believe that we can really begin the process of persuading and showing them that there is a different way to treat people." Marvin taught me that whenever you are in a difficult situation with someone, use the techniques described in our *CORE Rules for*

Action pamphlet—which specifically lays out procedures for interaction with an opponent. (CORE's papers are at the Wisconsin Historical Society.)

Marvin also taught me that you have to give your opponent an opportunity to save face. Give them a way out of the situation without belittlement. As Malcolm X and I debated back and forth, he made statements, I came right back at him, and countered, explaining what a CORE person would do in that situation.

When the debate ended, some callers agreed with me. Others did not. However, I thought I did a good job presenting CORE's point of view, further publicizing not only the sit-ins and freedom rides, but CORE's underlying philosophy for promoting political and long-lasting social change.

Years ago, I was contacted by a man who listened to my debate with Malcolm X on YouTube. I was shocked for many reasons. First, I had never heard of YouTube. Second, I tried for years to obtain the debate transcript but was told it wasn't available. I contacted Broadcast Pioneers, the organization in which Ed Harvey, the debate's moderator, had been active. I reached out to the Philadelphia Radio Archives without luck. I called the Schomburg Center for Research in Black Culture in New York City. I contacted the Homberg Library at the University of Maryland and the American Archives of Public Broadcasting. The Paley Center of New York City was my most recent attempt. I was unable to find a transcript. So, I just couldn't believe it.

In retrospect, when I listened to the debate on YouTube, I discovered that much was omitted. The YouTube clip is twenty-three minutes long, whereas the actual debate and call-in portion was slightly less than an hour. I suspect that whoever acquired the tape and created the transcript censored parts of it. For example, the debate was posted on YouTube on June 24, 2016, by the Disciples of Malcolm X, a group of his followers that included Elijah Muhammad, Clarence (13X) Smith, and Louis Farrakhan. They supported him in his heyday before Malcolm X made the life-changing trip to Mecca.

In his *Autobiography of Malcolm X,* Haley underscored that Malcolm was amazed when he went on his first pilgrimage to Mecca, which all Muslims are supposed to do, and encountered White people treating Black people as equals. He couldn't believe this, because he had not been in a situation where White people treated and accepted Black people as equals. During the debate, I predicted he would have such encounters in the future.

In an exchange, left out of the YouTube version, Malcolm X argued, "Evie, in this country, there have traditionally been what we call 'house niggers' and 'field niggers,' and they are pejorative terms of course for

Blacks and our history of slavery and oppression. The 'house nigger' worked for the White man in his mansion and the 'field nigger' worked for the White man in the field planting the crops and harvesting them, and that has been our history."

I remember stating, "Yes, that has been our history, Malcolm, but this is 1961, and now we don't have 'house niggers' and 'field niggers.' We have old Negroes and new Negroes." I continued, "The 'old Negro' continues to accept discrimination and segregation, while the 'new Negro' is leading a movement, asserting his dignity, his respect and his willingness to fight for right and justice. We must make a choice; what are you going to do? Are you going to be an old Negro or a new Negro? I'm a new Negro! What kind of Negro are you?"

I remember that vividly, more than sixty years later, because he was speechless, pulling himself together to respond. Malcolm X and I, along with the audience, had a very interesting interchange, very little of which is in the debate as it currently appears on YouTube. When I first listened to the debate years ago, Eustace Gay, the third man, was listed as a participant. But when I listened to it a second time later, Eustace Gay's name had been removed. The caption says, "Malcolm X debates Evie Rich." I therefore wrote to WCAU requesting the full transcript but was told that it is unavailable. I will try again.

I returned to my mother's home in positive spirits. We had dinner, and I caught a bus back to New York City. Marvie asked, "So, how do you feel about the debate?" I replied, "Well, I think I did okay. I didn't let him intimidate me." I then promptly forgot all about it. Almost sixty years later, I realized that I had successfully challenged the indomitable Malcolm X.

Malcolm X was assassinated on February 21, 1965. Clarence (13X) Smith was assassinated on June 13, 1969. Elijah Muhammad died on February 25, 1975. Louis Farrakhan is still alive. Malcolm X rightfully remains a great leader in African American history and in the civil rights movement. Yet, ordinary people like me have also played our small parts. Over my ninety-two years, I have had many adventures. The debate with Malcolm X is surely one of them.

2

Falling In Love and Correcting the Freedom Rides Record

Who would believe that during the fight against racial discrimination, so evident in the 1950s and 1960s, I would fall in love with and marry a White man! All the odds were against it, but it happened anyway. Let me back up and tell you that story.

I joined Students for Democratic Action (SDA), the student affiliate of Americans for Democratic Action (ADA), in 1950 on my first day as a freshman at Bryn Mawr College. SDA was founded in 1947 by Eleanor Roosevelt and others as a liberal political organization dedicated to building a just society through education and political advocacy. I was recruited after delivering a brief speech—given to meet the speech requirement for graduation—opposing the McCarren-Walter Immigration Act of 1951.

I met my future husband, Marvin Rich, in 1955 at a dinner party organized by SDA alumni days after I moved to Washington, DC, to take up my duties as executive secretary (director) of SDA. These SDA alumni—including Marvin—knew one another from their years in the student organization supporting liberal principles and programs. They were part of a newly organized ADA-led campaign to verify the end of de facto segregation in DC public facilities (following an Executive Order promulgated by President Dwight Eisenhower). Marvin introduced me to Wally Nelson, a CORE field secretary, who joined the ADA campaign in early 1956, infusing it with CORE's landmark principles of nonviolent direct action.

Marvin was a founder of St. Louis CORE, as well as St. Louis ADA. Born into a working-class Jewish family in St. Louis, his parents emigrated from Hungary at the turn of the century after the St. Louis World's Fair. Although his family was extremely conservative, Marvie held different views. Attending segregated schools, a vegetarian and a loner, he spent his free time reading. He had many brothers and sisters, as he explained to me, because in the Jewish religion children were prized. If a spouse dies, the surviving spouse remarries to provide a father and mother to the children. Marvie's father was a widower with three children who married a widow with three children. Then they had Marvie and his sister Rosie. Marvin had two brothers named Harry—Harry Rosenbloom and Harry Rich.

Enrolling at Washington University after graduating from Soldan High School, Marvin fell in with a group of veterans returning from fighting in World War II. It was 1946 and his new friends—some had lost body parts in overseas battles "to save the world for democracy"—could not fathom a segregated university refusing to enroll Negroes.

He immediately joined the Student Committee for the Admission of Negroes (SCAN), soon linking up with veteran student members of Teamsters' Local #688, which initiated—along with CORE—the struggle to integrate public facilities in St. Louis. I was wary of the Teamsters due to their reputation for corruption and violence. When I learned that Marvin was a Teamster, I backed away, telling him that I did not associate with bad people. Marvin assured me that Local #688 was different. Led by Harold Gibbons, the local was progressive and in the midst of challenging policies and practices that discriminated against Negroes. Today, St. Louis and its metropolitan area are still bad places for Blacks. Imagine what it was like at the end of the 1940s.

After receiving his AB (Artium Baccalaureus) in 1950, Marvin was active in the trade union movement, participating in various Teamster-CORE projects to desegregate St. Louis's public facilities. Preparing economic briefs for submission to the Wage Stabilization Board, he served as an organizer, research analyst, and administrator for the Teamsters at both local and national levels. He chaired the Teamsters Democratic Rights of Members Committee, as well as the committee that wrote the Teamsters' Plan to desegregate the St. Louis public schools. He taught nonviolent resistance at the Kentucky Labor School.

In 1955, he moved to Washington, DC, to work as a researcher for the Teamsters Union in its new building, which he termed "The Marble Palace." Reporting to then-president Dave Beck, Marvin immediately reached out to his old friends in SDA. Our small group, augmented by local DC ADA members like Charlie Mason, coalesced to conduct regular tests of public facilities in Washington during the fall, winter, and spring of 1955–1956. Restaurants, movie houses, theaters, swimming pools, bowling alleys, etc., we tested them all. The picket lines we encountered did not last long before the offending facility's resistance faded, and it quickly accepted compliance. We were official troublemakers.

I met Charlie Mason in 1954 at a New York City meeting about race relations in the Church sponsored by the Unitarian Universalist Church. A budding SDA activist, I attended events, meetings, demonstrations, picket lines, conventions, etc., organized and executed by progressives in the metropolitan Philadelphia area.

Marvie, Charlie, and I became a threesome. Charlie was the quintessential WASP—White Anglo-Saxon Protestant. He was very tall with blue eyes and gray hair. Raised by a maternal aunt after his mother died, he was an only child born into a Boston family of privilege. Charlie had three degrees from Harvard, including a bachelor's degree in engineering and two master's degrees. His engineering degree was awarded in 1933, while he earned a master's degree in applied physics in 1934. Charlie's liberal family raised him with progressive ideals. He was working in the US Naval Research Laboratory in DC when we met.

I liked Charlie from the first minute. A bachelor, he wore Boy Scout shoes, rumpled suits, and carried his green bag wherever he went. I learned from Charlie that Harvard undergraduates packed their paraphernalia in these green bags—books, pencils, and whatever. Long after Charlie graduated, he still carried that green bag.

Charlie Mason, Marvin Rich, and I tested restaurants, theaters, bars, and other establishments. Sometimes we met for lunch to test a restaurant. Members of our team, usually David Williams, who was editor of the *ADA World*—ADA's official newspaper—would join us. At other times we ate at Scholl's Cafeteria, one of the few integrated cafeterias in DC, offering wonderful, home-cooked food at reasonable prices. Remarkable by today's standards, we recounted what we ate at checkout and Scholl's calculated how much we owed.

Sometimes Charlie and Marvin would come to my apartment for dinner. We had very simple dinners, followed by games of Scrabble. Marvin almost always won because he knew more words than Charlie or I did. Marvin read everything, which came in very handy when we were fundraising for CORE. He knew where the money was! Charlie became a very good friend to both of us.

Marvin frequently tried to hold my hand when we were on our way to a picket line or demonstration. I shook it off, warning that he was making a big mistake and should stop. I stated, in no uncertain terms, that I was and would always be a career woman and would never, ever get married. I also made it clear that Whites and Negroes did not marry. Marvin said that he understood but still kept trying to hold my hand. (An important part of my philosophy is that you pick and choose your fights. This was not something I even considered fighting.)

It went further than that. I was highly active in the national and international student movement, representing the Students for Democratic Action on the Young Adult Council, affiliated with the National Social Welfare Assembly. The confederation of YAC domestic student groups included organizations like the Collegiate Council for the USA, Young Christian Workers, NAACP Youth Council, and, of course, SDA.

Invariably, when I traveled alone to New York City for a YAC meeting, Marvin would appear at the first session as an observer. He said that he really loved me and wanted to share in my adventures. I replied that he was out of his mind. Marvin followed me to Oberlin, Ohio, to an international meeting YAC hosted in early 1956, and later to Ohio State at the annual meeting of the National Student Association (NSA).

Back in Washington, Marvin showed such dedication and commitment to our work, calling out individuals and institutions which discriminated against "Negroes," that I couldn't believe it. He was always there, ready to participate, without excuses and willing to put his life on the line.

When the Teamsters transferred Marvin to Chicago, I was devastated. I did not want to admit that I liked him. Marvin called every day. He assured me that he would find a way to return to DC, and he did. I don't know how he achieved it, but when he returned, I admitted that I was really happy to see him again.

That's when the other shoe dropped. Not only did Marvin declare that he loved me but he also said he wanted to sleep with me. I said, "I have never slept with anyone and only married people slept with one another." "Not a problem," he said. I responded that I was on my way to Paris to a NATO Youth Conference and then on to Berlin to a meeting of the World Assembly of Youth as a YAC delegate, so he would have to wait. He said waiting was not a problem. I admitted that I really liked him very much but feared getting married. I did not want to lose my independence and would not give it up.

He replied, "You can be married and still have your independence. I'm willing to wait to share the rest of my life with you." Marvin and I were married later that year, in September of 1956.

My family accepted him. His family—with the exception of one sister (Rosie) and her husband (Milton)—did not accept me. Long afraid that Marvie would marry a non-Jew, they were horrified that he was marrying a Christian Negro. They asked Marvin's good friend to call me on the morning of the wedding to declare that they would never, ever accept me. (They ultimately did accept me, perhaps ten years later, through the intervention of their children.)

SDA friends who were available attended the wedding, which took place in my minister's home, along with our very small reception at my mother's house in Philadelphia. We drove to New York City the same evening and spent the night in a tiny apartment Marvin rented on Manhattan's East Side while I was abroad. We were married sixty-two years when he passed away in 2019. I was, then, and still am crazy about him!

As newlyweds, we joined and became very active in both the local CORE group and National CORE as well. Marvin got a job with a very good friend, Greg Bardacke, as Assistant Director of the American Trade Union Council for Labor Israel—the American support group for the Histadrut, which represents trade unionists in Israel. I went to work as Executive Director of the Student League for Industrial Democracy (SLID), the student affiliate of the League for Industrial Democracy, a successor of the Intercollegiate Socialist Society with the goal of addressing problems of poverty, housing, child labor, etc. Whenever Charlie came to New York City, he would visit Marvie and me (and later Gordon, our son). In 1959 Marvin left his job with the Israeli Federation of Labor (Histadrut) and went to work for National CORE as its Community Relations Director. CORE activities continued—both at the local and national level.

These activities included demonstrations (for example, at American Airlines), picketing (Macy's), and leafleting (*Daily News*). We were everywhere—Clinton Hill, Palisades Amusement Park, the Stork Club, etc. We focused on discrimination in housing, employment, and public facilities—and passionately pursued those issues. We also published two key pieces of literature: *This Is CORE*; *CORE Rules for Action*; and *Cracking the Color Line*. Jim Peck, a pacifist and active CORE member, edited the official newsletter, the *CORE-LATOR*. We distributed this literature to CORE chapters around the country.

On February 1, 1960, the s*it hit the fan. College students sat in at a Woolworth's dime store in Greensboro, North Carolina. CORE had no part in that original action, but the students went to the head of the local NAACP chapter for help. He had just received a copy of *Cracking the Color Line* and shared it with them, calling CORE in New York City for additional copies. A national movement was emerging with CORE at the center. CORE reached out to young people and their friends from chapters across the country. Soon there were sit-ins across the South, in the Midwest, and California.

Two CORE field secretaries, Gordon Carey and Tom Gaither, originated the idea of the Freedom Rides, extending the Journey of Reconciliation Freedom Rides

CORE initiated in 1947. The 1961 Freedom Rides and Freedom Riders electrified the nation in their effective onslaught against de facto interstate travel segregation, which continued despite the Supreme Court's landmark 1960 decision in *Boynton vs. Virginia.*

Before CORE took action, it always had a series of training exercises. In this case, they first selected the Freedom Riders—there were thirteen of them. They also chose "observers." Then they went through a rigorous training program in nonviolent direct action. Freedom Riders were testing the Supreme Court decision to ensure that integration of public facilities in interstate commerce was enforced. The plan was to depart from DC, and, through a series of pre-arranged stops, end up in New Orleans, Louisiana, where CORE had its strongest, most effective chapter. (New Orleans CORE members often said they were ordinary people doing extraordinary things.)

The afternoon before the Freedom Rides were to begin, Marvin went to the Trailways Bus Station and the Greyhound Bus Station in DC to purchase tickets. However, clerks on duty at both refused to accept his checks. Marvin called me—I was in New York—and reported, "Evie, I have a big problem. I tried to buy tickets for the Freedom Riders, but they would not take my checks because they were drawn on a New York Bank.

The bus stations will not accept checks drawn on out-of-District banks. What should I do?"

I said, "Marvie, it's very simple. Call Charlie Mason and convey the challenge. Remember, there are no problems; only challenges and opportunities. You tell Charlie to write checks on his bank for the Freedom Rides." So, Marvin phoned Charlie, and these two Caucasians rushed to the bus stations to purchase tickets.

No one knows this story, that Charlie wrote the checks for the Freedom Rides. His checkbook—a big, loose-leaf notebook—was in the green bag he carried everywhere. The Freedom Rides would have evolved, but surely started later and encountered a host of problems. Charles N. Mason Jr. financed the beginning of the Freedom Rides.

Charlie continued his good work in Washington, DC, marrying a dynamic African American woman named Hilda Howland when he was fifty-seven. Charlie always said that he became a husband, father and grandfather when he married Hilda. Our friendship with Charlie continued through many years until his death in 2006.

* * *

My first interaction with John Lewis was not a personal encounter. John joined the group of thirteen original

Freedom Riders in 1961. Marvin selected him, but I knew who he was long before we met because of his involvement with the Student Non-Violent Coordinating Committee (SNCC) and his expertise in nonviolent strategies. John Lewis was among the youngest of the thirteen original Freedom Riders when the bus left DC. Lewis was a mentee of Martin Luther King Jr., the foremost American spiritual leader in nonviolent actions. He also spent time with Jim Lawson, an iconic figure in SNCC. His knowledge, commitment, and experience with nonviolent direct action were key factors in his selection.

Rock Hill, South Carolina, was an early stop on the trip. We had a CORE chapter there. Tom Gaither, a leader in that group, was one of two CORE field staff championing the idea that CORE should initiate and then execute the Freedom Rides. But when the bus reached Rock Hill, riders were attacked for the first time. John Lewis was beaten very badly. John's White partner, Albert Bigelow, continued the ride. Rejoining the group at a later stop, John was sitting next to Albert when the bus reached Anniston, Alabama, where they were attacked by a huge crowd, including Ku Klux Klan members. Throwing firebombs inside the bus, they beat Freedom Riders as they escaped.

The following morning—this happened on Mother's Day in 1961—the *New York Times* featured a photograph of the Greyhound Bus fire in Anniston, Alabama, on the front page. The injuries sustained by Lewis and Bigelow were so severe that both were hospitalized.

Our relationship with John Lewis continued after that. Occasionally he traveled to New York on various speaking tours for SNCC, his primary affiliation when chosen as a Freedom Rider. Chairman of the Student Nonviolent Coordinating Committee from 1963 to 1965, he's renowned for leading the landmark Selma March in 1965. ADA's national headquarters was in Washington, DC, where Lewis resided from 1987 until his death in 2020.

We worked closely with him during the two years he served as chairman. Marvin was treasurer of ADA at the time, and I was a member of the National Board. Cooperating in a variety of ways, we testified before congressional committees, attended conferences and conventions, and organized and supported local chapters in their grass-roots activities—including the design and execution of the annual ADA Voting Record. Every year since its inception, ADA has identified twenty key votes on a wide range of social and economic issues—domestic and international—compiling a Liberal Quotient for each member of Congress. ADA publishes this data in its ADA Voting Record (which appears on its web site). John Lewis likely received a perfect voting score every year he remained in Congress. Elected to the United States House of Representatives for Georgia's Fifth Congressional District in 1987 and reelected sixteen times, he served until his death in 2020.

My last encounter with John Lewis was in 2017. Over the years, CORE contributions to the Freedom Rides have been documented, and movies were made. A 2017 film called *Freedom Riders: The Civil Rights Musical* featured historic events leading up to the Freedom Rides and their aftermath. I attended a showing hosted at the Acorn Theatre in New York in August of 2017. When I arrived, John Lewis was there. It was a tiny theater with a very small audience. Perhaps fifty people were present, but none were aware of John Lewis. I recognized him, and he recognized me. I said, "Gee Whittakers, I didn't know that you were going to be here, but I'm really thrilled to see you!"

I introduced Lewis to the audience. They recognized his name as I said, "This is John Lewis, the congressman from Georgia, who was one of the original Freedom Riders," indicating how lucky they were to be in the presence of this iconic man who had such a powerful impact on civil rights in the United States. John and I sat together to view this film, and I subsequently wrote a review of it.

I was not at all impressed because, as I said in my review, "As a musical, it is a paean to SNCC, the Student

Non-Violent Coordinating Committee, and it also celebrates one of the most significant social movements of the 1960s. It makes up for in wonderful music what it lacks in authenticity. It leaves the Congress of Racial Equality (CORE) on the sidelines. CORE originated the Freedom Rides and participated through their conclusion as hundreds of riders were gradually released from Parchman Prison Farm when the US Government finally guaranteed free and unfettered access to interstate commerce via ICC regulations." Basically, the music was wonderful, but the musical omitted facts as they really occurred. Leaving a great deal open to question, it should be challenged.

This happened again at John Lewis's funeral. There was reference to the Freedom Rides, but no mention of CORE. Those on the sidelines are waiting for a revision of the still-current "script" that rightly credits the Freedom Riders and their cause, while overlooking those who conceived and persevered in creating this movement. Nevertheless, I especially salute one young, iconic freedom rider—John Lewis.

3

Funding the Sit-ins and the Freedom Rides

Thomas Paine, the Revolutionary War pamphleteer, writes in "Common Sense": "They also serve who only stand and wait." This sentence resonated the first time I read it decades ago. It still does because it reminds me—vividly—of all those who helped raise early money for the sit-ins and the freedom rides, ordinary people whose contributions changed the face of the nation. Their small acts of courage, contribution, and sacrifice were harbingers of larger, far more influential acts to come. Many waited to be told what to do next. But most were truly engaged in these small acts.

To guarantee both authenticity and accuracy, I consulted the definitive text, *CORE: A Study in the Civil*

Rights Movement, 1942–1968 by August Meier and Elliott Rudwick. I also looked at Ray Arsenault's *Freedom Riders: 1961 and the Struggle for Racial Justice.* To my surprise, neither book mentions crucial early funding for the sit-ins and freedom rides so richly part of my personal experience. I was on-site and they were not, nor were their sources present during the action.

Claude Sitton, a *New York Times* reporter, wrote about the first sit-in in mid-February 1960. Sitton described how a group of Negro college students were refused service at the lunch counter at the Woolworth's Five and Ten Cent store in Greensboro, North Carolina. His article made the front page of the *Times*. Almost immediately, Marvin received telephone messages at the CORE office from callers asking what they could do. Rich and poor, Black and White, young and old phoned. New York CORE's membership tripled overnight. Sitton, a Southerner, spent four years reporting on incidents involving both the sit-ins and the Freedom Rides.

As I wrote in Chapter 2, Marvin left his job with Histadrut, an affiliate of the Israeli Federation of Labor, to work as a full-time CORE fundraiser in 1959. He did so to support CORE's nonviolent action program adopted by a growing number of CORE chapters across the country.

Over the next several months, a number of young sit-in participants visited New York City. Youth on the front lines were so important to our movement. In the South, high school and college students braved hoses, dogs, and other efforts by law enforcement personnel to discourage any and all kinds of early support for our activists. Simultaneously, CORE members met with potential donors on Long Island, Westchester, and other parts of the Metropolitan area. Money slowly arrived but it was only a trickle compared with what was to come. Yet it was a beginning.

Student actions resulted from the production and distribution of *Cracking the Color Line*, which Jim Peck, a New York CORE member, took the lead in producing. None of our New York CORE members had any money. Among the earliest founders of CORE, Jim Peck, editor of the *CORE-LATOR*, was the wealthiest. But you would never know he had a penny.

When I met Jim at an early NYC CORE meeting in 1956, he was married to Paula Peck, an outstanding cook whose two books, *The Art of Fine Baking* and *The Art of Good Cooking*, brought her national recognition. Marvin and I were members of Washington, DC, CORE, so it was only natural that we linked up with the local CORE group when we moved to NYC. (Marvin had met Jim long before, and they were close friends.)

Peck's family owned Peck and Peck, a women's specialty store on Fifth Avenue in New York City, perhaps the equivalent of Bergdorf Goodman, which specialized in women's classic clothes. There were a few branches in other cities as well. Yet Jim wore rumpled suits and Boy Scout shoes. As far as I know, Jim never made substantial financial contributions to CORE. Indeed, it was CORE's activism that absorbed his interest and energies.

Jim Robinson was the acknowledged leader of the NYC CORE group. (He was a student at the University of Chicago when CORE was founded.) Although small in number, the New York City group pursued several activities, holding meetings on 42nd Street in a space rented by a local union. I recall these efforts vividly because we rented clothing reflecting the issues we wanted to highlight. We hired evening gowns to picket nightclubs, Santa Claus suits for picketing Macy's, and bathing suits for the Palisades Amusement Park in New Jersey. We picketed the latter because Negroes were denied access to their pools. Macy's, Gimbels, and Saks Fifth Avenue department stores were singled out over their refusal to hire Negroes as sales personnel. The Stork Club and other New York nightclubs were targeted for their refusal to admit Negroes.

However, *Cracking the Color Line*, the project led and pamphlet produced by Jim Peck, put New York

CORE in the spotlight. Peck had a long history of activism when he joined CORE. He was a former seaman and one of the founders of the National Maritime Union. A conscientious objector (CO), Peck was arrested more than sixty times during his lifetime for participating in acts of civil disobedience reflecting his beliefs and, in my view, his leadership. Long after his expulsion from CORE by advocates of the Black Power movement, Peck continued opposing the Vietnam War, the potential use of nuclear power, and many other issues which absorbed his attention.

Peck authored *Cracking the Color Line* with assistance from other CORE members. Martin Luther King wrote the introduction. Highlighting various nonviolent options in a range of situations, the pamphlet provided the spark for CORE's proactive involvement in the sit-ins. The NYC CORE group mailed *Cracking the Color Line* widely to like-minded groups across the country. One such group was the NAACP chapter in Greensboro, North Carolina, whose student members initiated the first sit-in. Chapter members were enthralled with the descriptions of CORE's nonviolent, direct-action techniques in cities across the country. Southern CORE chapter students launched their own sit-ins, and the Woolworth campaign was off and running with little clear direction or financial support.

CORE had very little money at that time. Lula Farmer, Jim Farmer's wife, was treasurer. To the extent that there was a direct mail program—and it was minuscule, if at all—Lula wrote stellar thank-you letters. Treasuring these letters, Marvin considered them on a par with John Kenneth Galbraith's appeal letters for Americans for Democratic Action (ADA) when Marvin oversaw ADA's direct mail operation. Local group activities generally meshed with those of CORE's national office. There wasn't a clear distinction. Charles Oldham served as president of CORE until the great schism of the mid 1960s, when a number of Black members rejected the concept of a White man serving as president of the group and even, for some, Whites playing prominent roles in the organization.

The sit-ins and their rapid success created a need for additional CORE staff and funds to pay them. This included students jailed or expelled from school—thus ripe personnel to augment CORE's small staff. Again, I'm not talking about large amounts of money. I'm referring to funds for picket signs, entrance fees to potential picketing targets, etc. Over the following years, our CORE staff grew astronomically and paying staffers was a challenge. CORE struggled to find funds to maintain its growing operations across the country, North and South. Remember, this was 1961, and no one was paid very much.

Raising money was key to CORE's success. I never knew how much Marvin raised. It's not that he hid it from me. Rather, it was because the need was so great. Coming from a humble family without money, attending college on a room, board, and tuition scholarship, Marvin excelled at fundraising, and I helped him. I learned a lot about fundraising in the process.

What I am attempting, however, to describe is where the early money came from and how it grew. This story is unique because CORE's goals—though ultimately to strengthen American society and showcase its democratic institutions—had a long way to go to achieve full-scale equality for Blacks and Whites. Movement toward those goals met with fierce resistance from the nation's financial institutions. Ronnie Moore and Kenny Johnson, two of Marvin's closest associates, were indicted and jailed for allegedly "stealing" some of the money. How much was involved I never knew. I do know that both emerged from that experience with reputations intact.

CORE jumped right in when the sit-ins began and responded to students' requests for help, organizing nonviolence workshops—since nonviolent direct-action techniques were obviously working. Marvin identified and cultivated a relationship with a commercial banker who served as a last-minute Santa Claus. When Marvin was desperate, he went to Santa Claus, who lent Marvin substantial funds without collateral. Marvin always paid him back. It was a private agreement between the two. On occasion, I asked Marvin how much Santa Claus loaned him, and Marvin responded that I didn't really want to know. Marvin finally revealed his identity but swore me to secrecy to protect Santa Claus's job.

We were challenging basic, long-standing, and highly regarded (although racist) institutions. They were not about to lend CORE money, much less *give* CORE any. There were small trickles here and there, but no substantial amounts appeared out of the blue. Student participants were hosted by our neighbors in Queensview West, the lower-middle-income cooperative where we lived. We had no money for hotels. Friends and neighbors fed them and chauffeured them to their various appearances, including speaking and television appearances that Marvin arranged. Others spoke at union meetings.

Most notable were the audiences invited by Dorothy Norman and a small coterie of her friends and associates. Dorothy Norman was an outstanding photographer, writer, editor, and supporter of social activist causes. Not only was she very good to all of us, but her son Andrew (Andy) followed in her footsteps as director of the Norman Foundation, which made substantial contributions to CORE, much of it underwriting legal fees for jailed riders.

Early funding for both the sit-ins and freedom rides derived from four major sources: wealthy, primarily Jewish, philanthropists; labor unions; direct mail solicitations; and small family foundations. Dorothy, for example, was from a wealthy Jewish family. Among women philanthropists who came to CORE's aid, Dorothy holds a special place. She—sometimes joined by her close friend, Lillian Smith—invited their friends for evenings with sit-in participants, and shortly afterward the Freedom Riders at her home on Manhattan's East Side. (Lillian Smith's controversial novel, *Strange Fruit*, traces the interracial affair of a prominent White Georgian and an African American woman in 1920s Georgia.)

The number of riders would vary, but she always had good food and lots of it. The riders described their adventures to a growing audience. At first, the sit-in participants and freedom riders were quiet and reticent. It was my job to make them feel comfortable. I told them about my adventures fighting discrimination, took them with me to 125th Street to picket Woolworth's, enlisted them to help neighbors in Queensview West paint picket signs, and exchanged the lyrics of rowdy college songs. Over months and years, we became good friends.

Also in that group were Jo List Levinson, Elaine and Jim Slater, and Katrina and Courtlandt Barnes. Albert List, a wealthy businessman, contributed significant funds early on. He lived in Greenwich, Connecticut, when Marvin and I met him through Jo, his daughter. Albert contributed substantial resources to CORE and so did his daughter Jo. And, like Dorothy Norman, Trini Barnes, and Elaine Slater, Marvin met them all via *New York Times* reporter Claude Sitton, whose almost daily accounts chronicled the activities of first the sit-in participants and then the Freedom Riders.

Among wealthy individual philanthropists, primarily Jewish, who identified with the struggle and contributed was Doris Chanin Freedman. Doris organized the first (and subsequent) CORE art shows, where the public could purchase significant pieces of art from outstanding artists of the day, including Andy Warhol, Philip Guston, Willem de Kooning, and Robert Indiana's famous poster, *LOVE*. Doris Freedman was a remarkable woman. Her grandfather built the Chanin Building across the street from Grand Central Station just before the beginning of the Great Depression. It is a New York City landmark and a classic example of Art Deco. The inside of the building with its various symbols is magnificent but, unfortunately, photos are prohibited.

Doris was ultimately responsible for the art shows' organization and execution. Stellar individuals from New York society served as chair and co-chair. Committee members represented New York's high society. Where

I have stressed the involvement of "ordinary" people in organizing and funding CORE, the five art shows she organized with her committee are exceptions. They brought a new dimension to CORE's fundraising efforts. The first CORE art show, "Artists for CORE," was held in 1961 and raised $40,000, a king's ransom by CORE standards. The Scholarship, Education and Defense Fund for Racial Equality (SEDFRE) helped students return to college, find new careers, and begin new lives.

The exhibits were designed to support both the sit-ins and the Freedom Rides. Well-known artists joined with up-and-coming artists to lend current works. They also produced new exhibitions for various galleries—first in New York City and then beyond—raising substantial dollars to maintain CORE staffers. Purchases also provided bail for hundreds incarcerated in southern prisons because of their participation in CORE projects. Doris Freedman went on to become NYC's Commissioner of Cultural Affairs and, significantly, influenced public art in the city.

* * *

Our struggle was not simply a Black struggle. It brought out so many caring White people. For many Blacks, their involvement had a lasting impact far beyond the actual money. Too many Blacks had never met White people who treated us as equals, who chose to join our everlasting fight to redeem our democracy. When the Black Power movement came along and destroyed the struggle or set us back for generations, few in our movement had met this type of White person. Told that White people are evil, the devil, the enemy—whatever—I simply fell back on my own experience because I knew it wasn't true.

Each of the women mentioned above called Marvin in the CORE office to ask what they could do. All had their hearts in the right place. Marvin asked them for money. More importantly, we asked them to take action—participate in our picket lines, solicit their friends, throw CORE parties, etc. And they did!

Jo List became one of my closest friends. We later traveled to Washington, DC, together to yell at the leaders of Emily's List (Early Money Is Like Yeast) for their refusal to back our candidate for Congress in the NY Fifth Congressional District. Emily's List officials insisted that Barbara Clark, a New York State Assemblywoman, had failed to raise sufficient money on her own. On yet another occasion, we tried to buy a house in Crown Heights, Brooklyn, as a refuge for abused Orthodox Jewish women, but the powers that be there would not permit it. Jo List died in 2001. I remain close to her son,

Daniel, who shares her commitment to social justice and action.

The Slaters were the offspring of Abe Wechsler, founder of Wechsler Coffee Company, who owned several up-scale restaurants in NYC, including Mama Leone's and Windows on the World. The first time Marvin and I visited them in Rye, New York, we mistook the garage for their home. They provided space at their restaurants for CORE fundraisers and picked up the tab. They became surrogate parents to some of the Freedom Riders and helped them meet tuition costs at the various universities the riders attended. Elaine Slater, at one hundred years old, is still alive and kicking. We still talk occasionally and relive old times. She and her husband Jim moved to Toronto when Richard Nixon was elected, because neither could abide by his presidency. Their children continue Elaine's and Jimmy's good works in many ways, and Elaine remains in close touch via email.

Today the Barnes' would be called a "power couple." They lived in a townhouse in Murray Hill, with additional homes in Aspen, Colorado, and Santa Fe, New Mexico. Trini's real name was Katrinia McCormick Barnes. I didn't know it at the time, but Trini's parents were elected officials. Her father, Medill McCormick, was a US Senator and her mother, Ruth Hanna, was a US Congresswoman. Trini brought confidence, commitment and service to the table in her own right. An heiress to a storied Chicago family, with close ties to the *Chicago Tribune*, Trini served on the boards of numerous organizations committed to social justice, including the ACLU and the Chicano Education Project. She also endowed a scholarship at the University of Denver for a minority student.

I had many adventures with Trini, and I miss her. She often invited us to dinner with her husband, Courtie (a.k.a. Courtlandt Barnes), a New York socialite she married in 1935. Courtie was also a Yale grad, a Wall Street stockbroker and a pianist. Marvin used to tell the story—I don't know how true it is—that when Trini married Courtie, she did not want to have more money than he did. She gave away money so that their assets would be equal. It appears that Courtie was a big investor in Seeing-Eye dogs. Courtie was also head of the Aspen Colorado Festival. Our son, Gordon, was a classical pianist, but Courtie told me that he would never be a first-rate pianist. Gordon continued to play but made music an avocation.

Trini and I were highly competitive when it came to cooking. Obviously, she had a lot more money, but I tried to make up in ingenuity what I lacked in resources. When the three of us—Gordon, Marvie, and me—visited Trini and Courtie in Aspen or in Santa Fe, I prepared spectacular dinners—for example, fresh salmon I brought with me on planes from New York. I made certain the airlines we flew on had refrigerators. Trini countered with equally competitive recipes like meatloaf with raisins and pine nuts. To my advantage, Aspen and Santa Fe supermarkets and grocery stores lacked merchandise available in New York City. We stayed in a guest house on their property in Aspen, visited with their friends, discussed our work, and planned next steps. In both cities, we spent time enjoying music—especially the Santa Fe opera.

Their funds were supplemented, as mentioned, by contributions from the Norman Foundation—directed by Dorothy Norman's son, Andrew. The Taconic Foundation, led by Stephen Currier, was also a contributor but, to my knowledge, to a far lesser degree. Audrey Hess and her husband, Tom Hess, invited their friends to add dollars.

As CORE membership in local chapters across the country grew, so too did the need for funds to support their activities. Meier and Rudwick describe these activities in detail in their book but overlooked the four key early funding sources cited above, including direct mail. Securing funding through direct mail was allotted to Marvin during his early tenure as CORE's Community Relations Director in 1959. Marvin also learned a great deal about direct mail as a member of the fundraising committee of national ADA, which organized and executed ADA's Roosevelt Day Dinner for local northeast leaders. Marvin helped recruit and sustain major ADA dinner contributors.

Marvin had a talent for direct mail. He purchased many books on the topic, talked with experts, tried various techniques to increase the "return on investment," and shared all that he learned with me. It paid off. As an aside, Marvin was a reader. He read everything. I still have some of his books. Coupled with mine, they cover our entire apartment. Whenever CORE and later the New School, Queens College, and Mercy College needed money, Marvin knew where to find it. Of course, knowing where it was is one thing. Getting it is another.

Important, too, was the early involvement of unions. Again, in my view, Meier and Rudwick ignored the key role progressive unions played in these early years. International Ladies' Garment Workers Union (ILGWU) leaders active in Americans for Democratic Action gave CORE money. Our long involvement with ADA—which still exists—introduced both of us as young students to the progressive/liberal establishment in this country. Our participation and roles changed over time, but we remain grateful for the opportunities extended, lessons learned, and the contacts made.

Gus Tyler, Charles (Sascha) Zimmerman, Shelley Appleton, and later Jay Mazur and other ILGWU luminaries visited Washington for ADA's monthly National Executive Committee Meetings. As SDA representatives, we were also there to listen and participate. Voting on the Executive Committee and National Board, we sat side-by-side with Arthur Schlessinger Jr., John Kenneth Galbraith, Reinhold Niebur, and Eleanor Roosevelt. They did not treat us like children, and we didn't act like children. Some of the nation's leading progressives, including labor leaders, emerged from those encounters. Marvin and I knew them, and we went to them for help with CORE.

Other unions involved included the nascent 1199 Hospital Workers, led by Leon Davis. Marvin developed long-term relationships with Moe Foner, leader of the cultural arm of 1199 via their Bread and Roses Cultural Project. Jack Sheinkman, president of the Amalgamated Clothing and Textile Workers; and Jerry Wurf of DC 37 of the American Federation of State, Council and Municipal Employees (AFSCME) also participated, as did the Steel Workers, along with the Machinists and the Mineworkers. Presidents of these powerful national labor unions sat at the table with us as we debated the issues of the day. Marvin and I reached out to all of them when we moved to New York City—especially those based in the city, but others through our membership in the Workers Defense League (WDL), which represents workers unfairly denied workman's compensation. We were all over raising money for CORE.

Sheinkman retired after negotiating the union's merger with the International Ladies' Garment Workers Union to form the Union of Needle Trades, Industrial and Textile Employees (UNITE). Leaders of smaller unions also made significant contributions. The Hotel Trades Council opened their doors to all Freedom Riders, as well as the Little Rock Nine. My point: The labor movement rallied to support both the sit-in participants and Freedom Riders. Not only did they contribute funds, but they also contributed bodies, spaces for participants to sleep, and, also vital, men and women for the picket lines.

CORE's aggressive actions in finding funds to support the sit-ins and Freedom Rides is an exciting story. It drew Marvin and me from our small, modest communities into an arena of people and organizations with large sources of money—willing to contribute to a cause we held in common. Wonderful human beings stepped up to the plate to help abolish segregation and discrimination in this country. Many became our very close friends. We learned so much from one another. Their early efforts set the stage and made possible the growth of CORE as it altered the civil rights fabric of our country.

4

African Adventures: Uganda

The majority of African scholars have PhDs in African studies. Numerous self-described radical scholars call the continent "Mother Africa." Less radical scholars call her "Black Africa." I believe the latter group commands more respect in the scholarly community. Still others like me simply call her Africa. During the period that Africa occupied center stage in my professional life (1966–1976), I worked with all such experts, first as a teacher, then as a teacher-scholar, and ultimately as an administrator. Many scholars look down on K-12 teachers, but I didn't let this bother me. I thought I knew as much about Africa as they did despite their extensive research.

My interest in Africa and the many African-related activities I experienced leading to my Uganda adventure did not happen accidentally. They began with Sundays at the Galilee Baptist Church in Philadelphia. We all went to Galilee on Sundays, except my father who, for most of the time I lived at home, served as choirmaster at other churches. My mother always said, "You sleep in my house on Saturday. You go to my church on Sunday."

Indeed, Galilee was my mother's church. Babies and children attended Sunday School in the church basement. The regular service began afterward. There were two collections: first, the Sunday Missionary collection, and then the regular collection. The Missionary Society was an important part of the church. Occasionally, missionaries visited, sharing their experiences in Africa, primarily West Africa and especially Liberia. A service highlight: when missionaries brought someone from Africa with them. The service was amended to permit the guest to address the congregation. He—almost always a male—would tell us about his life, dreams, and aspirations.

This went on for years. Additionally, we subscribed to the *Philadelphia Tribune*, the Philadelphia newspaper catering to Negroes. I voraciously read their articles about Africa and Africans. Mother, who attended Tuskegee High School and Voorhees Junior College (now Voorhees University)—both historically Black schools—was highly knowledgeable about Negro history. She told us about

Marcus Garvey and his "Back to Africa" movement. Our minister, Reverend Frank B. Mitchell, graduated from Lincoln University, a historically Black college (HBCU), now a university. His classmates included such famous African celebrities as Kwame Nkrumah, the first president of Ghana, and Nnamdi Azikiwe, the first president of Nigeria.

Over meals my mother recounted facts illustrating that Negroes not only could but also did achieve at high levels. Later at Bryn Mawr Black reunions (there weren't many), Black alumni complained about the absence of Black Studies in the curriculum. I often pointed out that I learned my Black history at home and in the church.

I was one of the few Black students in Students for Democratic Action (SDA) during my years at Bryn Mawr. Another Black SDA member, Walter Carrington, certainly influenced me, although the level of influence is debatable. Wally (as we then called him) was from New England, attended Harvard as an undergraduate, and attended its law school when I first met him in SDA. We were both active in the Young Adult Council and participated in World Assembly of Youth (WAY) meetings in Berlin and Delhi. Wally worked for the US federal government when he finished law school.

After graduating from Bryn Mawr, I was deeply immersed in the Congress of Racial Equality (CORE).

Moving to New York City, Marvin and I were active in CORE programs. We also maintained contacts with like-minded organizations such as the Fellowship of Reconciliation (FOR) and the War Resisters League (WRL), where membership often overlapped with CORE. Simultaneously, we continued ACLU membership and joined the Workers Defense League (WDL).

I went to work as a teacher of social studies at the New York City Board of Education in 1962 after Marvin revealed one night that CORE wasn't paying us. He said CORE had so many people in the field that there just wasn't enough money to go around. Teaching at a middle school across the street from our co-op presented an opportunity for steady income and new educational horizons.

After the Russians launched Sputnik in 1957, the US government was motivated to fund graduate courses in wide-ranging "area studies" at a host of universities, including Columbia University in New York City. Columbia featured a vibrant African Studies program. For the first time, however, the government offered Columbia grants to recruit additional students in African Studies, and that's why I didn't have to pay for the courses I took. I took as many courses as I could and, with the blessing of my supervisor, introduced the first course in African Studies at the John Bowne

High School where I was teaching. Africa soon became a major area of interest for the US government. In the late 1960s, collaborating with a friend from the Young Adult Council, we produced an innovative textbook on Africa—*Africa: Tradition and Change*—published by Random House in 1972.

It's against this background that in 1972 I was offered a job at the African American Institute, a nonprofit organization then located in New York City. I had just completed the coursework for my PhD in African Studies and Education at Columbia University after taking a year's leave of absence from teaching. I wasn't certain if I would return to my teaching job in NYC or write my dissertation.

Marvin, who was a truly wonderful man, very creative, and so different from me, had just left a position at the New School for Social Research in New York City where he raised money for good causes. He fell into development, which is another name for fundraising, because he'd spent most of his adult life in the Civil Rights Movement. He became CORE's leading fundraiser because the organization needed money. Marvin went on to spend his entire professional career as a fundraiser. After leaving CORE, Marvin went into business for himself with another gentleman, Martin Schneider, raising money for good causes like the NAACP, and

ASPIRA, a Hispanic group focusing on high school students. These organizations sorely needed funds for operations. Realizing this, both he and his partner rarely paid themselves. Having finished my coursework, I intended to return to work. How did we survive on such limited income? I was an expert at stretching dollars and finding bargains, as well as a terrific cook.

I was offered a job with the African American Institute, whose major goal was to inform Americans about Africa, and to promote African development. My teaching experience certainly was relevant and Wally Carrington, now Walter Carrington, was a vice president of the institute. I received my introduction to the African American Institute through young Americans who were involved with Africa. And as an active member of student and youth organizations in this country, I traveled abroad to international youth conferences where I met youth from African colonial territories. I developed close friendships with a number of them.

All this leads up to my position at the African American Institute in 1972. My interest in Africa was first generated at church, expanded at home, and further honed when I met young men and women at these international conferences. One of the institute's missions was to instruct teachers in American schools how to teach about Africa effectively.

In 1960, numerous African countries won their independence from European Colonial rule, and American interest in Africa blossomed. In ensuing years, the African American Institute created several programs designed to bring African students to the United States for both undergraduate and graduate degrees in American universities. It hosted conferences where Africans played leading roles. It also produced periodicals and pamphlets on a host of Africa-related issues.

Around 1970, the African American Institute created the School Services Division to teach American students about Africa. I was appointed director in 1972. My qualifications were many. I introduced the first African history course in the New York public school system, traveled abroad extensively, and I co-authored a well-regarded high school/college textbook about Africa with Immanuel Wallerstein, a friend and scholar at Columbia University.

But I had never been to Africa. However, I made a point in my interview to stress that teaching Americans effectively about Africa required on-site African experiences. With funding from the Carnegie Corporation of New York, the African American Institute launched a program called "Educators to Africa." The concept: to provide American teachers with on-site experiences so that they could develop curriculum materials that emerged from authentic involvement with Africa and Africans.

AAI indigenous African representatives met on-site with Mel Johnson, director of Educators to Africa, to design a program for visiting teachers that would give them authentic exposure to the countries we visited. In 1972, I took American teachers from around the country on a six-week trip to Africa with the purpose of designing curriculum materials for implementation in American schools. The participants received six graduate credits from Howard University and a free trip to Africa. We went to Ghana, Togo, Dahomey (now Benin), and Nigeria in West Africa before flying to East Africa.

I had twenty-eight teachers with me. They were White and Black, young and old; in fact, some were college professors. They ran the gamut when it came to knowledge about Africa. Some knew nothing. Others fell into the category of "radical African scholar" or "less radical" African scholar. Several knew a lot about Africa. Others thought they knew everything! As their group leader, this presented both challenges and opportunities. For the most part, we were based at African Universities. Accommodation was adequate, although by no means luxurious.

For example, there were complaints about the absence of hot water in the showers at the University of Cape

Coast where we stayed, or the repetition of the food we were served—lots of plantains and chicken. However, there were also more serious situations, such as visiting slave castles like Elmina off the coast. Exposure to the dungeons where slaves were kept while awaiting the Middle Passage understandably riled up the radical scholars, who refused to speak to the White participants for several days. Some burgeoning friendships were destroyed as a result. I pointed out that—while not excusing the slave trade—surely they must be aware that slavery existed in Africa long before the arrival of the Europeans, although it was a very different kind of slavery. I also noted that there were obviously African collaborators who facilitated the trade. This did no good. These scholars did not listen to me. Rather, they insisted that I was making excuses for the White man.

During our visit in West Africa, Ghana's first president, Kwame Nkrumah, died and we all went to his funeral. Death is an occasion for celebration in Ghana, rather than mourning, since the deceased is now making the journey to join the ancestors. The deceased is returned to his/her place of birth. Mourners wear red and black in Ghana.

Another event was especially interesting to me. West African women wear wonderfully colorful clothing. In 1972 there were no department stores as we have them here. Rather, there were Singer sewing machines. In the villages we visited, one would seek out a seamstress, select the material from an array of choices, be measured, and return the next day for the finished product. When we were about to leave, one of the local women explained that she would like to exchange her dress for my dress. I readily agreed. I had several dresses made while there (the turn-around time was so quick) and was delighted to add her dress to my collection. I still wear several at appropriate times.

After we spent about three weeks in West Africa, we flew to East Africa, specifically to Ethiopia, Kenya, Tanzania, and Uganda. I personally had a great time in East Africa despite a disturbing experience in Uganda. At the University of Dar es Salaam in Tanzania, our group met with Walter Rodney. A Guyanese scholar-activist, Rodney was a strong critic of capitalism, and had just published his most important, widely acclaimed book, *How Europe Underdeveloped Africa*. The radical scholars in our group were delirious. The book dissects the history and negative impact of slavery worldwide, extols socialism, and champions ordinary people and their role in promoting political, economic, and social change. A spokesperson for global liberation movements, Rodney became persona non grata in his native land as his recognition and influence grew in the Caribbean as well as Europe and the Americas. He was assassinated in Guyana in 1980.

Our group also spent a couple of nights in the Ngorongoro Conservation Area, a protected UNESCO World Heritage Site located in the Ngorongoro District, an arm of the Tanzanian government. The site is named after the Ngorongoro Crater, created when an active volcano cone collapsed inward, leaving a large caldera or bowl-shaped volcanic cavity. Considered one of the Seven Wonders of Africa, Ngorongoro attracts tourists anxious to view firsthand the world's most extensive collection of large mammals, including buffalo, elephants, lions, and more.

This was one of the highlight experiences of my life. I told Marvin that we had to visit it together—and we did—several years later. In 1972, Uganda was ruled by Idi Amin, a Ugandan military officer and politician who served as the third president of Uganda from 1971 until his overthrow in 1979. Considered one of the most brutal despots in modern world history, the film *The Last King of Scotland* portrays him as the military dictator he was. He was cruel. There were numerous Asian merchants in Uganda. Idi Amin didn't like Asians, but he hated White people even more. Not only did he dislike them intensely, but he murdered them. And our itinerary included Uganda. To be honest, AAI did not anticipate the emergence of Idi Amin when the itinerary was drawn up.

I really didn't like the idea of going to Uganda with twenty-eight teachers, nearly a third of whom were White. Daily newspapers were filled with stories of Idi Amin and his hostility to Asians and Whites. I called the office in New York, spoke with my supervisor, and said that I didn't think it was a good idea to take these teachers to Uganda. He said, "You have to," and I responded, "It's not safe; it is absolutely dangerous, and we are putting these teachers in danger." He replied, "It's on the itinerary; you have to go." So I took this group to Uganda.

The capital of Uganda is Kampala, and the international airport is located six miles south of a major city called Entebbe. (In 1976, Israel launched a counterterrorism mission known as Operation Entebbe in response to the hijacking of an Air France civilian flight to Tel Aviv, successfully rescuing all the hostages.) At thirty-nine, I was leading a mixed-race delegation of teachers to a country that was hostile to Whites and Asians. It was my first visit to Africa, but I was in charge of a potentially life-threatening situation.

I decided that the only way to leave Uganda safely was to get out when I went in. What does that mean? Idi Amin was killing White people. I had to get all of us out safely; the emphasis was on *all*—if I left White people there, they could die. The challenge was to be creative, to do something differently. I have great confidence in my ability to convince people to honor my requests.

It was particularly imperative to make a positive impression on the key customs official, as well as the bus driver who would pick us up and take us back to the airport. My plan: To ask these two figures to speak to our group about their life adventures. Before we left for the trip, I printed up business cards that said *Evelyn Jones Rich, New York, NY 10017* and bore the African American Institute logo.

Landing in Entebbe, naturally we went through customs. I collected the passports of all our members and said to the customs agent, "I am so thrilled to meet you. You probably have the best job in all of Entebbe because you meet so many different people, beginning with me. I am Mrs. Rich from New York City." Handing him my business card, I continued: "I want to introduce you to my team, one at a time, and I want you to give each of them their stamps." I introduced each to him as they passed through and he stamped their passports.

Then I said to him, "We are here to learn about your wonderful country, and we want you to come to our hotel and give us a lecture. We have already lined up outstanding leaders to talk to us—university professors, tradespeople, merchants, but *you* are the *most* outstanding, and we want you to give us an inside view and tell us all about your adventures!" He said he would be thrilled to come.

Once we passed through customs, a prearranged bus took us to our hotel. Boarding the bus, I told the driver, "What a great job you have! You are carrying distinguished people out of the airport into Kampala, I bet you have a lot of stories to tell us. We are here to learn about your wonderful country and would like you to come to our hotel and give us a lecture; we have already lined up outstanding leaders to talk to us—university professors, tradespeople, merchants, scholars—but *you* are the *most* outstanding, and we want you to tell us about your adventures." He said he would be thrilled. Soon we arrived at our hotel.

When these two men came to talk, I told our teachers to ask many good questions. "We must pretend we're really interested." Their lectures were, in fact, interesting, because the questions were insightful. We had nice refreshments—the whole nine yards. Not only did I bring my business cards on this trip, but I took something else that ended up being very handy when we needed "something special": one hundred one-dollar bills. For example, we couldn't drink the tap water in Uganda because no one knew what was in the water. I would give a Ugandan five single dollar bills to find bottled water for us.

We spent five days in Uganda, visiting Makerere University and various other places. The night before we left, then–US Ambassador Thomas Melady hosted a reception for us. It was held outside on the grounds of his beautiful home. But he warned me, "Evie, you will never get out of this country." I said, "You wait and see, oh yes I will."

At the last minute, one of our members fell ill and I rushed her to the hospital. She had a terrible gallbladder attack in the middle of the night. The dollar bills I carried served a good purpose that evening. But before leaving I told the women in my group that they must wear dresses during our journey home. I warned, "You may not wear pants, you must wear a dress; and I want you to pack sanitary napkins inside your suitcases on the very top; go to the store and buy some." Airport officials had a reputation for going through luggage and throwing belongings all over the place. At some point during our visit, we went to an American commissary where I purchased four bottles of scotch whiskey. I kept those bottles close at hand. The political situation was tense.

I went to the bus company the night before we left, met the driver and his supervisor, and told them, "We're looking forward to our trip to the Entebbe International Airport." I gave the supervisor a bottle of scotch, and he was thrilled.

The bus driver showed up at 6:00 on the morning of our departure, and we all boarded the airport bus. I handed him one of my remaining bottles of scotch. I had also asked the customs man to meet us and lead us into the airport. At that point, I still had two bottles left. I said, "We are so happy to see you. We enjoyed your lecture so much." The airport was chaotic, and he led us to his station. I smiled and said, "We're going to come through and want you to give us our departure stamps; you remember everyone!" All the women wore dresses as instructed. He let us through and stamped the passports.

I told him, "We'll meet you in the lounge." There were now twenty-seven of us because the teacher remained in the hospital, but she was African American and wouldn't be harmed. If she were White, I would not have left her behind. After we passed through the customs area, I said, "We're going to open a bottle of scotch while we wait for the plane, and we're going to give you a bottle!" I don't even like scotch.

When customs officials opened our suitcases and saw the sanitary napkins, they immediately closed the bags because they were embarrassed; that was the idea. When we entered the lounge, we opened a bottle of scotch; we each had some as I brought paper cups. Finally, it was time to get on the plane. When the others were safely onboard, I gave the customs man the last bottle and then climbed the stairs to the plane.

I have never in my entire life felt such exhilaration and joy as when we boarded that plane. Flying to Athens to refuel—we didn't get off the plane—we spent the night in Brussels on our way back to New York. I am now ninety-two years old. One of the first book collections Marvin and I purchased was Churchill's volumes about World War II, including *Their Finest Hour.* In my lifetime, I've had many, many adventures, but when I strode into that plane safely with twenty-seven teachers and the door closed behind us, it was definitely my finest hour.

* * *

Uganda was only the beginning of my leadership at AAI teaching and learning about Africa. Over the next four years, I faced one challenge after another. My extensive African background provided a foundation as I tackled assignments I loved. Unfortunately, the majority of African scholars argued that Africa had no history, no achievements, no luminaries, nothing to celebrate—that Africans never invented anything, notwithstanding the stone walls at Great Zimbabwe. Prominent scholars at the time also insisted that Egypt wasn't in Africa. It was in the Middle East. I knew better, and my staff and I set out to prove it with AAI's full support. Blacks look to Egypt as a crucial part of our culture and heritage.

We challenged the vocabulary that scholars and teachers use to teach about Africa. We took hundreds of teachers to Africa for an on-site African experience. We then visited those teachers in their home schools and helped them implement the new curricula they developed based on their African experience. We evaluated existing materials about Africa. We showed teachers how to use poor, ineffective, and often inaccurate texts, films, articles, and other information about Africa effectively. We introduced them to concepts underlying the oral tradition—long used in Africa.

We tapped into an important first line of offense by hosting a conference, "The Passionate Librarian's Guide to Africa," introducing librarians to valid new and more effective materials about Africa. We joined local, state, and national educational bodies to convince them to include questions about Africa on local Regents, SAT, and ACT exams as a strategy to infuse the study of Africa in the curriculum. Over a period of four years, we energized teaching and learning about Africa. We created our own materials to supplement those available tapping into new scholarship about Africa. Conversely, we worked with African governments, universities, and schools to demonstrate how to shake off colonial pedagogical practices and introduce African students to learn about and appreciate their own history, environment, and culture.

I left AAI in 1976 to write my PhD dissertation and returned to teaching at the NYC Board of Education. My ties and contacts with Africa and Africans remained strong. Marvin and I hosted Africans under the US International Visitors Program or several private programs which brought Africans to America for study or site visits.

* * *

In 1996, I received a Fulbright grant to take twelve elementary and secondary teachers on a six-week curriculum development journey to South Africa. This was in the aftermath of Nelson Mandela's release from prison and his subsequent election as president, coupled with the decline of apartheid. South African discussions typically stressed apartheid, whereas its decline changed the entire picture. Details of that visit will have to wait until another time. However, it did not have the drama of the 1972 trip to Africa years earlier. Further, our group was more cohesive in the sense that there were no radical scholars.

The American Committee on Africa (ACOA) and the Phelps Stokes Fund—two nonprofit organizations long associated with Africa—sponsored our trip, although the Fulbright Program picked up the bill. Because of both organizations' close ties to Africa, our trip was far more political—visiting women's groups in the apartheid resistance movement, political party meetings, as well as K-12 schools and universities. We focused on Cape Town, Durban in the East of South Africa, and Johannesburg, a.k.a. Joburg, perhaps its most famous South African city.

We spent most of our time in the townships located just outside the cities because during apartheid, for the most part, Africans were not allowed to live in the cities. For me the highlights were school visits where I presented lessons illustrating how we teach in the United States as compared with the teacher/recitation method prevalent in English-speaking Africa. Students were impressed when I used Michael Jackson's "Thriller" to teach about Halloween, for example.

The African groups we interacted with were anxious to showcase the progress they were making. We visited a school with an accounting class. I was delighted and asked the next logical question, "What about jobs for graduates?" During this visit, I noticed the name of an American accounting firm on the door of a nearby office building. I found the phone number and requested an appointment. At that meeting, I suggested the firm hire a few of those local accounting students and they did! Developing countries should look for opportunities to help their students, and I was trying to show South Africans how to move forward. I pointed out that all of us must look for opportunities—sometimes right under our nose.

I am disappointed in the lack of progress African nations have made toward embracing democracy. The continent has certainly nurtured outstanding leaders. The majority of Africans I met over fifty years shared my view of nation-building with democracy as a vital base. It is never too late to make a significant move toward building a free society for its people.

5

Girls Do Carry Papers

"You want to be a *paper girl*?" The man in charge of delivering the *Philadelphia Inquirer* looked at me incredulously. "Paper girl," he repeated, as if I were out of my mind. "There is no such thing as a paper girl. Boys carry our paper. There are only paper *boys*. Girls don't carry papers."

"Of course they do," I responded. "My brother is a paper boy, and I want to be a paper girl. Also, I need the money. Collecting empty bottles for deposits isn't enough. It costs ten cents to go to the movies where Negroes are required to sit in the balcony, and I don't have the money to go. Where does the Constitution say that girls can't carry papers?"

I landed the job as a paper girl with my own route. It was 1944. I was eleven. The newspaper cost three cents, and I was paid half a penny for each paper delivered. I took to the job with relish. A year later the price of the paper rose to five cents, and I received a penny a paper. I stood up for myself with an adult man and won. I had the means to earn money. I felt victorious!

I don't have clear memories of my first four years of life, but according to family history, we lived with my father's mother and some of his siblings in a large house on Terrace Street in Roxborough, a section of northwest Philadelphia. Our nuclear family consisted of my mother, father, my older brother (Carleton), my fraternal twin sister Barbara, my younger brother James Jr., whom we called Tot, and me. My father's mother, Jennie Reavis Jones, the matriarch of the family, owned the residence. When the Great Depression hit, her home was foreclosed, and we were all evicted.

I have no idea how my parents were able to move the six of us into that small house in West Philadelphia. I suspect that my enterprising grandmother helped organize it. My earliest recollection is studying morning glories in the backyard. It was 1937, and I was about four years old. Like the morning glories, I awoke early. Scanning the flowers, I counted the new ones since the day prior, marveling at their deep purple color. I wore a yellow sweater all the time because it was the only sweater I owned.

My memories of living in this house are mixed. I recall hiding under the bed in an upstairs bedroom whenever a representative from the hospital arrived. He was a regular visitor. I hid under the bed because I feared he would take me back. I don't remember being in the hospital but was told that I had malaria. In retrospect, this is confusing since I was never exposed to mosquitoes that carry the disease. Luckily the hospital's representative, who was actually collecting money toward the hospital bill, never took me back with him.

My father was a musician. He earned a living playing the piano (I don't know where), organizing male music groups, and organizing and directing church choirs. He had little or no work during the years we lived in West Philly but was helped by the Works Progress Administration. The WPA was a federal government program created to help families survive the Great Depression. We were all on welfare. I vividly remember having very little to eat during those years. Oatmeal for breakfast, lunch, and dinner. To this day I refuse to eat oatmeal and cornbread. Hominy grits were a welcome alternative. With butter it wasn't all that bad. Sometimes on Friday we had fish. I adore fish. It represented a change of pace from oatmeal. I looked forward to dessert. When there was money, we had rice pudding, tapioca pudding, or bread pudding with raisins.

I learned how to read at an early age and read all the time. My twin sister, Barbara, was a more typical child; she didn't read at such an early age. When Barbara and I went to kindergarten in February 1939, the teachers—all White (although the neighborhood was Black)—were shocked at my ability to read and comprehend.

Barbara and I had our own language. We understood each other. When we went to kindergarten, the teachers insisted that we attend speech class. I looked forward to speech class and practiced the pronunciation teachers introduced. I was also a troublemaker. For example, I spoke to Barbara in our special language, or I wrote on the blackboard and imitated what the teacher was saying. I interrupted the lesson and ordered the other students to do something. Barbara followed me, carrying out my instructions. The teachers talked about separating us but never did. Ultimately, we lost the language we spoke, and I recall none of it now. But I have continued to observe the morning glories in my current backyard, closely following their gradual opening, reaching out toward the full sunlight and then slowly closing at night.

When I entered third grade, my grandmother was somehow able to buy back the big house on Terrace Street in Roxborough that she had lost in the Great Depression. The six of us moved back in with her. Her two daughters, Beatrice and Genola (GG), and three of her grandchildren also lived with us. The house was large, but you could never tell it from the front. It was built on a hill with two stories in the front, but four or five stories in the back. There was a basement where we never wandered, a kitchen level, living room level, bedrooms on a third story, and an attic. We kids—there were seven of us by then—slept in the attic with Aunt GG's three children on one side and me, my sister, and two brothers on the other. As far as I can remember, the house had one bathroom for all eleven of us. Nevertheless, the interior was beautiful.

I don't know how long my grandfather, Bill Jones, lived with my grandmother. He was a carpenter. When he lacked employment, Bill worked on the house, installing molding on the walls, French doors on all the openings, and new paint throughout. He created a space in a room below for my grandmother to execute her numerous projects. My brother, Carleton, inherited his talent for fixing things. Indeed, there were few things that Carleton could not fix. My younger brother, Tot, was also very handy.

The settling and development of Roxborough, along with the adjacent areas of Manayunk and Wissahickon, is a fascinating story of urban growth in the years following adoption of the US Constitution. Modern Roxborough, once part of Roxborough Township, was incorporated into the City of Philadelphia after the Act of Consolidation was passed in 1854. The old Roxborough was an area of millers, tradesmen, and farmers. The Schuylkill River in its course through Manayunk attracted businessmen for its potential waterpower and ease of transportation. The area, particularly Manayunk, played an important role in the early industrialization of the Mid-Atlantic States, facilitating economic, political, social, and religious change. The completion of the Schuylkill Navigation Company's Canal in Manayunk in 1823 transformed the textile industry, brought in working-class laborers from England and Scotland, and made Philadelphia an industrial center. The owners of the textile mills of Manayunk lived in Roxborough, making it a wealthy part of Philadelphia.

Roxborough, Manayunk and Wissahickon were and remain an area of hills. To negotiate these hills, early settlers built steps. This was very strange to me because I had seen steps in a house but never outdoors in a community. There were steps everywhere. Often to go from one street to another, one had to negotiate a pair of stairs and, in many instances, they were very steep.

Manayunk is now an upscale community which is hardly recognizable from the old days. The old five-and-dime store is gone. In its place is an upscale shop on once seedy Main Street, bracketed by trendy stores of all kinds. Shops, restaurants, and other expensive business places line the canal on both sides. I could hardly believe it when I returned after many, many years. One street over, the Proper Brothers furniture store is still there.

When our family returned to living with our grandmother in Roxborough, my siblings and I went to Levering Elementary School whereas all the other Black kids in the neighborhood—which was integrated—went to Joel Cook Elementary. Our mother, who had attended segregated schools, felt that a school that served White children would deliver a quality education. She was skeptical about the staff, curriculum, and students at Joel Cook Elementary. So my assertive mother met with the superintendent of schools and somehow managed to get all four of us enrolled in Levering Elementary. And that is how our adventures as the only Negro kids in a White working-class school began.

Back then, the school year was organized into two semesters: A and B. School authorities separated us. Barbara went to Class 2B, and I went to Class 3A. We were about eight or nine at the time. I loved school. I did my schoolwork, read a lot, and managed the jobs I had on the side. Since money was scarce in our household, my siblings and I figured out ways to make money.

My first job before landing the paper route was house cleaning. Every Saturday I wiped the wooden table and chairs in the kitchen of my employer. Then I scrubbed her kitchen floor. I made a dollar every Saturday. Since that was good money, I held the job for quite a while. I gave it up to be a paper girl.

My younger brother Tot and I sometimes exchanged paper routes and occasionally covered for one another. We threw the papers in the recipients' front yards since there were no apartments in Roxborough. We did this seven days a week. I was eleven in 1944 at the height of World War II. Tot was nine and a budding entrepreneur. He had multiple ways to make money whereas I was more limited. For example, Tot rose early in the morning, captured night crawlers, put them in jars, took them to school, and charged other students a penny to look at these creatures. Tot had our mother make a tuna sandwich for his lunch. Just before lunch, he would unwrap it so his classmates could smell the tuna. Then Tot would sell half of the tuna fish sandwich for a nickel.

My best job was working in Mr. Jimmy Bulllock's fruit and vegetable store on weekends where I made five dollars. Mr. Jimmy lived in our neighborhood and was a Negro entrepreneur. He hired me because I had a reputation for being smart and trustworthy. I worked in the store for many years—even when I was a college student. Not only did I feel rich, but Mr. Jimmy would give me leftover unsold merchandise that I brought home for family meals. I learned a good bit about fruits and veggies in the process. This was during World War II, and like many families, we had a victory garden. Our family shared a garden up Ridge Avenue in the Andorra section of Roxborough with my mother's day-work employer. We grew everything we could in our victory garden, including veggies I considered "White people's food"—such as Swiss chard and leeks.

Mr. Jimmy, who also had his own vegetable garden, sold some of it in his store: white sweet potatoes, eggplant, squash, etc. The best (and maybe worst) thing about working in Mr. Jimmy's store was the fish. Every Thursday night Mr. Jimmy went fishing off Cape May, New Jersey. He caught lots of fish, primarily bass and porgies. We sold the fish on Friday. My job—in addition to waiting on customers—was to clean the fish. I would cut off their heads, split them sideways, and remove the insides. Mr. Jimmy often gave me the leftovers. I took them home and my mother cooked them for dinner.

My siblings did not want to sit next to me at the dinner table because they said that I smelled like fish. That didn't bother me at all because I was a loner, spending my spare time reading or attending the Green Lane Public Library. Early on, the library had a Wednesday afternoon story hour. The librarian would either read us a story or tell one. I loved that and read my way relatively quickly through the children's section. The librarian picked out books for me to read in the adult section. Unfortunately, her knowledge of the great classics held there was paltry. I read a lot of mediocre mysteries, although I did read a few good ones.

Cleaning kitchen furniture, carrying papers, and working in the fruit and vegetable store were not the only jobs I had as a youngster. My point is that I was not proud. I needed the money and any job I could find that was legal appealed to me. Throughout the years, until I graduated from college, I also worked as a contingent, wherever I was needed at John Wanamaker's in Philadelphia. I also sold dresses in a small store in the same area. While in college, I served as a fire captain in the dormitory, a paid position.

I had a fierce desire to be independent, a willingness to take risks, and refused to accept limitations, and—most important—refused to live the life seemingly carved out for me. There had to be something better out there. I didn't know what it was, but I was determined to find out.

* * *

In 1946 we moved from my grandmother's house into a small house in Wissahickon, a different section of

Philadelphia. I don't know whose idea it was. In retrospect, I think it was my grandmother's. Why my mother agreed to move her family away I do not know. However, she refused to move unless the bathroom, which was then a toilet in the backyard, was brought inside. My brother, Carleton, collaborated with someone to achieve this goal by dividing the third back bedroom in half, creating a wall and installing a tub and toilet.

I was thirteen when we moved into that small house on Dexter Street (later renamed Manor Street), where we were one of four Negro families. The house was very small, but the six of us squeezed in. My mother and father shared the front bedroom, Barbara and I the middle bedroom, and Tot and Carleton slept on a bunk bed in the back bedroom. Ashamed of the house, I did not want anyone to know I lived there. The street was not paved. On the few occasions when I was dropped off by someone with a car—probably from church—I insisted that they leave me on an adjacent street or avenue. I then walked home. Years later, Carleton knocked down the walls between the living and dining room on the first floor, creating a single space. The house also had a basement which was above ground level where the furnace was located. We played cards there. As I indicated above, I loved school. I enjoyed studying, invested the time, and was rewarded. The second semester of seventh grade and all of eighth grade are vague in my memory. In grade 7A, both boys and girls spent a morning at Roxborough High School. The boys received instruction in Industrial Arts and the girls took cooking and sewing. It was an effective introduction to high school, which we all attended from grade 7B until graduation.

I continued being a loner, until ninth grade, when I joined a group of White students—primarily female. We were considered the smartest kids in the academic course. There was intense competition. I felt that the teachers—all White—were prejudiced. Roxborough High School served all the kids from Roxborough, Manayunk, and Wissahickon. Since our family moved to the small house in Wissahickon, we were then living farthest from the school. It took a while to walk. Bus passes didn't exist. You walked or didn't go to school.

When I tried out for the annual play, *Our Town*, I was told that there were no parts suitable for me. According to the assistant principal, the play focused on a White family and there could not be Negroes in this family.

While in high school I became a co-editor of the school newspaper—*The Ridge Record*—and joined the debate club where I was ultimately elected president. Most of all I enjoyed participating in extracurricular music groups—the a cappella choir and various choruses—evolving from my participation in music groups at my church (Galilee). I did not have a great voice. I was a second soprano. My sister, Barbara, was an alto with a much better voice. Father created our own singing group, and we belted out spirituals at occasional ad hoc musical events.

Times were hard financially for our family. This was 1946. My father did not bring his salary home. Occasionally he gave my mother $20 to feed all of us. I believed he was selfish, spoiled, and thought only of himself. For that I hold my grandmother responsible.

These experiences helped me understand that college required an academic scholarship (there was no affirmative action) and succeeding meant changing the world for everyone. I told myself that I would never get married and subject children to the life I was living. Recognizing the dilemma my mother faced, I thought she was wonderful. Mother dropped out of college to marry my father. She had four children but no financial resources on which to depend. She worked as a domestic—a cleaning lady—to raise the money to feed us. My father bought the coal to heat the house in winter, but this is the only remembrance I have of his support. I recall the many occasions when my mother asked my brother, Tot, to catch fish in the canal for dinner. Or when she encouraged us to pick wild blackberries for a dessert pie. We had lots of lima beans, fresh corn, fresh tomatoes, and homemade biscuits for dinner from our victory garden. The fish was wonderful.

Our father was rarely home while working with his various musical groups. He told us that he worked at the Philadelphia Navy Yard off and on as a draftsman. He did not like to get his hands dirty. When he lost that job, he worked briefly at another where he had to wear clothes that got dirty. Although mother washed his garments, he resented having such a job in the first place.

I spent those years primarily reading books from the Wissahickon Public Library. By that time the Roxborough Public Library had closed. I lost myself in the adventures of Nancy Drew, the Hardy Boys, etc. Totally unaware of the great writers, I concentrated on murder mysteries and nursing stories. I was especially intrigued with the adventures of Laura Ingalls Wilder and her vivid descriptions of a life of struggle in the cold of the Dakotas. I was always cold in winter because we did not have enough warm clothes to wear. We often put winter coats on the bed to keep warm. I'm still cold in winter in my very warm clothes.

During my early years at Roxborough High, we earned letter grades. I was always "distinguished." This meant that at report card time, I received either all As or all As and one B. If a student had more than one B, he/she was meritorious. This changed my senior year when grades were calculated numerically. I was in stiff competition to be valedictorian, along with a friend and competitor who was White and, in my view, wealthy. Looking back, her parents were probably not rich. It's just that they had more money than mine, and mine had none.

College was always on my mind and that of my friends in our academic peer group. All ended up attending what I now would call second-tier schools. As valedictorian, I was able to obtain free tuition at any accredited school in Philadelphia. I chose Bryn Mawr, because on weekends my mother often cooked and served dinners for wealthy White women on Philadelphia's Main Line. I often helped her wash dishes. One of the White women told me about Bryn Mawr—also located on the Main Line. A catalogue, a visit, and a supplementary scholarship for room and board from the National Scholarship Service and Fund for Negro Students (NSSFNS), closed the deal. I was off to my next adventure—the first Black working-class student at Bryn Mawr to live on campus rather than attending as a non-resident, commuter student. Bryn Mawr changed my life.

6

The US Post Office: Mama's Bank

God Bless the United States Post Office. My grandmother had great respect for the Post Office, which was what she called the United States Postal Service. And so do I. We called her "Mama," but my grandmother's real name was Jennie Reavis Jones Joyner Wormley. Her life was inextricably bound up with the Post Office. I reject current efforts to privatize the Post Office and so would Mama if she were still alive. Mama was dependent on the Post Office, as were millions of low income urban and rural people across the country. This is as true today as it was in the 1940s, perhaps more so. Although I doubt that Mama ever visited our neighborhood Post Office, she sent me there regularly.

Congress created the Post Office banking system in 1910, primarily to serve low-income people and new immigrants. More affluent people also used it as a backup for their regular bank. In its heyday the Post Office held almost three billion "banked" dollars. Congress abolished this feature in 1966, when higher interest rates and the introduction of the Federal Deposit Insurance Corporation made commercial banks more attractive. I'm certain that commercial banks were thrilled.

Born in North Carolina, Mama moved to Philadelphia with my grandfather, William Jones, and her four children—part of the African American south to north migration following World War I. As I wrote above, our family of six lived with her in a large house in the Roxborough section of Northwest Philadelphia. So did my three cousins, their mother, and occasionally another aunt. We referred to the home as 4312 (for its address) and still call it that. Although no longer in the family, it holds cherished memories.

Mama was the matriarch of our family. What is amazing is that she was illiterate. I can only speculate as to how she raised the money to purchase the house in the first place. She worked three jobs. First, she was a hairdresser. My grandfather, Bill Jones, constructed her shop from a large space inside the house. Mama was always busy doing hair at three dollars a head for neighbors and members of the community. I frequently joined in the conversation—usually asking questions. Customers occasionally found my questions annoying, but I pointed out to all that questioning was the key to learning. They didn't like that, but Mama did not tell me to shut up.

She was also a domestic worker, cleaning homes for a specific amount—from $5 to $10 a day depending on the size of the house. I still have memories of my brothers bringing home a china closet or pieces of fine furniture one of her "madams" had given her. She placed it in the living room where we were not allowed to sit. Over the years, Mama created an attractive living room filled primarily with vintage furniture.

Finally, Mama was an inventor. She invented the recipe for her special "Jennie Joyner's Liniment," which she sold in four-ounce bottles with labels I designed. Mama stood over the stove at night, stirring a pink liquid that smelled somewhat like camphor, and sold her secret concoction for a dollar per bottle. People said that it worked. By then she had divorced my grandfather and married Mr. Joyner. I do not recall his first name and rarely saw him. He did not live with us.

When I was nine or ten, I started "banking" for Mama at the Post Office—depositing and withdrawing cash stashed in brown paper bags. I was already recognized as the "scholar" in the family. My mathematical skills were exemplary, and I handled the basic calculations with aplomb. Mama knew this. She was illiterate, but highly intelligent.

First, I completed the pre-printed deposit receipt—typically several hundred dollars. Mama reminded me to keep a supply of deposit and withdrawal slips on hand. Then I walked to the Post Office where I deposited the funds. When I complained about the danger of walking around with a paper bag full of money, Mama assured me that no one would imagine that there was money in the bag.

Mama was superstitious. For example, she would not let anyone pass her on the stairs. There were many of us and a large number of stairs. But Mama was adamant. It was her house, she told us, and we would do what she told us. We didn't challenge her. We followed her instructions. Years later, when I was the principal in a high school with 3,000-plus students, it was difficult at first for me to use the stairs when students went from one class to another. Since I was usually in corridors and stairwells while they were in the building, I had to overcome this resistance to passing people on stairs.

Mama liked me. Perhaps not as much as my older brother, Carleton, but she admired my intellect and ability to hold my own in conversations with other people, especially older adults. I would read to her at night—primarily astrology books. Mama was a Scorpio but knew all the signs of the Zodiac. She listened intently and often insisted that I reread a portion. Associating signs with people she knew—including customers—she pointed out personality traits justifying the Zodiac sign she attributed to them. If I noted why it didn't work in a particular case, she shrugged it off.

When the astrology book stated it was time to make a move, Mama directed me to make a withdrawal. I completed the appropriate form, walked to the post office, withdrew the money (sometimes several thousand dollars), and gave the money to Mama in a brown paper bag. Mama had already phoned her lawyer, Edward Polisher. I then accompanied her to his office, where Mama bought another house. Each home cost from nearly a thousand dollars to perhaps two or, rarely, three thousand dollars. They were in different parts of Philadelphia. I have no idea how Mama found or made the decision to buy them. All of Mama's business deals were referred to as "big time."

I was embarrassed that my very business-savvy grandmother marked an "X" on documents certifying the sale. So I convinced Mama to let me teach her how to write her name. She had trouble with the "J," since it can be written in two different ways, yet insisted on learning how to compose the more difficult representation of the letter. Imagine the lawyer's surprise the first time Mama wrote "Jennie Joyner" in large, sprawling letters. I was very proud of her, and I told her so. I felt good that she relied on and trusted me.

Mama died young of a cerebral hemorrhage after a short hospital stay. She was fifty-seven. I was sixteen. At the time of her death, she owned six or seven houses. She left the big house to her son, Elmer, and daughter, Beatrice. I was shocked to learn that Mama left the secret liniment recipe to Elmer, but have no idea what he did with it. I do know that Elmer never made any liniment.

* * *

Many people are unaware of partisan efforts to put the Post Office out of business, yet seniors like me and rural residents still rely on it. The Post Office is the largest US employer after Walmart, employing approximately 625,000 people; a large percentage are minority workers. The US Postal Service is required not to lose money, even though it must deliver mail to areas that are unprofitable: for example, processing a letter mailed in Hawaii addressed to Florida at first class rates represents a loss of revenue.

The US Postal Service lost $26+ billion over recent years. Direct mail advertising, a major part of its business, generates an estimated ten billion pounds of waste annually. The Post Office struggles to compete with the significant increase in alternative delivery systems including FedEx and United Parcel Service (UPS). Not to mention that emailing, texting, and inexpensive phone service are a much more immediate means of communication than writing letters.

In this environment, efforts to put the Post Office out of business gain even more traction. I can imagine explaining this to Mama. A congressional mandate requires the Post Office to prepay billions of dollars into retirement funds for future Post Office retirees, an annual deficit of around $5 billion. This is coupled with a decline in first class mail, a significant increase in less profitable junk mail, the recent elimination of 212,000 jobs, as well as the closure of delivery routes and processing plants. New proposals include trimming pensions, combining paid leave with sick days, and reducing delivery services.

All this explains why I admire the United States Postal Service. In addition to all the services the Post Office provided when I was very young, it was Mama's bank. It met her needs and served her well. It should return to being—among other things—the banker for powerless minority and immigrant people like Mama. Her entrepreneurial actions left a lasting impression on me. I like to think that I learned a lot from Mama and the United States Postal Service.

I suggest that Congress authorize the Post Office to return to its former role as the poor people's bank. It could potentially break even and stop partisan efforts to destroy it. Then I would hear Mama telling me that it's time to make a move—from my big commercial bank to the US Postal Service.

7

Galilee and Me

My mother led us to church every Sunday morning. As we approached the sanctuary from a few blocks away, we could hear the music . . .

> Oh come, come, come to the church in the wildwood
> Oh, come to the church in the dale
> No spot is so dear to my childhood
> As the little brown church in the vale . . .

Written in the mid-nineteenth century by William Pitts, the "Little Brown Church" hymn has been sung by congregations across the nation throughout the years. We sang it often in Church—usually as part of the regular service rather than as a processional or recessional. "No spot is so dear to my childhood as the little brown church in the vale," epitomizes my feelings about Galilee Baptist Church of Philadelphia, which we simply called "Galilee."

Galilee still stands on the corner of Roxborough and Mitchell Street in the Roxborough section of Philadelphia. It is and always has been a Black church in a White neighborhood. Today, developers probably have their eye on the large property consisting of the main building and a parsonage next door with a large backyard. Although educated in the public schools of Roxborough, I was also educated in the Galilee Church for the seventeen years I spent there. Galilee significantly shaped the person I am today.

Baptists founded the first church in Roxborough in 1789, followed thirty years later by the Methodists. Galilee was first organized in 1896 to serve the small Black community in Roxborough, Manayunk, and Wissahickon when a group of African Americans met for services regularly in the home of a Mr. Graham. They later moved to the second floor of a house on Walnut Lane and Pechin Street. Mr. Graham became the first pastor. They named their church Galilee Baptist after Mr. Graham's former church in Virginia. Religious services were held in members' homes or schoolhouses.

Assisted by Rev. Horace B. Wayland, pastor of the Zion Baptist Church in nearby Germantown, Galilee began holding services and building a congregation like a regular Baptist Church. A succession of pastors followed, including Rev. Royal H. Brown and Rev. Clarence Parrish, who was ordained and installed on July 2, 1899. The founding members purchased the property on the southwest corner of Roxborough Avenue and Mitchell Street. The cornerstone was laid in 1900.

Deacon Taylor and Deacon Wesley McCullough supervised the church's construction. I remember Deacon Taylor vividly when I was growing up. Sitting in a pew in the front of the church, he seemed like a very old man. On the first Sunday of each monthly Communion, his hands shook as he folded the Communion cloth to begin the ceremony.

The church was built in stages as funds became available. Galilee's services were moved to the just completed basement of the church in August 1901, with the simultaneous organization of a Sunday School, a one-room ungraded school. The house next door was purchased sometime during the 1930s and Sunday School was moved there. The church building was completed during Reverend Parrish's tenure.

Galilee experienced rapid growth during the early decades of the twentieth century. The Tribe of Benjamin—an organization like the Missionary Society but with younger members—and a Baptist Young People's

Union (BYPU) were formed. Other activities followed in future years. The church was carpeted. Toilets were moved inside. An organist was hired. A Junior Choir was formed. In November 1918, the mortgage was fully paid off and ceremoniously burned. The church was closed temporarily that year due to the flu epidemic. In early 1919, the church was fully wired and a new organ was installed.

Roxborough—like most urban cities—remains racially segregated. However, from its earliest settlement it embraced a special kind of segregation. There were small areas only for Blacks, but also sections where Black families lived side by side in semi-detached homes surrounded by White neighbors. Largely a working-class/lower-middle-class area with churches, businesses, homes, it also features a cemetery where Blacks are still buried in the back. In its heyday—the 1930s through the 1960s—Galilee boasted a membership in the hundreds. Members, representing all ages, participated fully in a range of activities led by groups that organized and conducted them on a regular basis. My mother was at the center of nearly all church activities. A mover and shaker, she saw a need and rushed to meet it.

Children and young people were an important part of life at Galilee. Activities for children included: Cradle Roll (where toddlers and babies were cared for while their parents attended services), Sunday School (before regular Sunday services), the Baptist Young People's Union (BYPU) and the Baptist Young People's Fellowship (Fellowship). The BYPU and Fellowship ultimately merged to become the "Fellowship." There were other occasional events, including "Tom Thumb" weddings—where youngsters from the Cradle Roll—up to maybe five or six years old, put on full scale "weddings"—and Christmas pageants with children reenacting the birth of the Christ Child.

Adult organizations included the Missionary Society, Men's and Women's Bible Classes, to name a few. My mother was a leader and ultimately president of Women's Bible Class #3. Bible class members organized numerous church events like Layman's Day, when former and present members who lived far away were urged to return for a day of prayer and remembrance. I was the Speaker on Layman's Day in 1990.

My mother and her church friends helped organize the annual Fourth of July parade—a big event showcasing all the churches in Roxborough, Manayunk, and Wissahickon with picnics afterward in designated areas of nearby Fairmount Park. Other regular church events included Founders Day, Men's Day, Women's Day, and Children's Day. Typically, church friendships became neighborhood friendships and vice versa. Women were the organizers and worker bees, not unusual for African American churches at the time.

Music was an important part of life in Galilee, both during services and at special events. Choir concerts often featured soloists. Choirs from other churches were invited to perform. Sometimes two choirs pooled members and sang together. And did they sing! They sang standard hymns from the Baptist hymn book, as well as anthems, spirituals, and gospel music. Music featured in other denominations was incorporated into our church music. For example, the "Little Brown Church on the Hill" is not a Baptist hymn. It has assumed universal acceptance and power. So too, have "How Great Thou Art," "Amazing Grace," and many others.

What is equally amazing is the role of the congregation in the church's music. Everyone sings: little children; pre-teens and teenagers; young adults and middle-aged parishioners; older members and senior citizens. I attended many church services throughout my lifetime. Congregants in White churches open their mouths. Congregants in Black churches sing with verve, enthusiasm, interest, meaning, and love. You can hear the Black congregation singing blocks from the church.

I vividly remember singing in various church choirs—chancel, youth, and regular choir. Several additional choirs were formed catering to specific kinds of music such as a Gospel choir. When I was in college, I often heeded my father's request to bring an alto or a first soprano from Bryn Mawr to enrich the singing at Sunday service. They hung their fur coats on our cellar door, shared my twin bed, ate my mother's bacon, cheese, and egg biscuits on Sunday morning, and joined the processional at church. They could all read music, and my father, who was choirmaster at Galilee for many years, was delighted. My twin sister, Barbara, played the organ.

Galilee offered Revival Services on an occasional basis. Designed to renew one's faith, revival was held over a week, often with a different minister preaching the sermon on one or two weeknights. Members came from Roxborough, Manayunk, Wissahickon, and from other parts of Philadelphia because of outward migration or the church's vibrant spiritual life. Except for revivals, refreshments featured nonalcoholic punch and homemade cake. All this happened against the backdrop of competition from two other Black churches in the area—Umbria Baptist and Josie D. Heard AME; so far as I know, neither still exist. I was always involved with Galilee, either as an active participant or leader.

Youth fellowship attracted me and many other young people on Wednesday nights. Reverend Frank B. Mitchell, whom we called "Rev," served as Galilee's minister from 1935 until 1950 during the entire time I attended Galilee.

Shortly after I left to enroll at Bryn Mawr College, Rev left to become pastor at Pinn Memorial Baptist Church where he was based for the next forty years.

Reverend Mitchell oversaw youth activities. A graduate of Lincoln University, he often regaled us with updates about his college classmates. These included famous African American poet and playwright Langston Hughes, Supreme Court Justice Thurgood Marshall, and Kwami Nkrumah, the first president of Ghana. Rev also interacted with Nnamdi Azikiwe, the first president of Nigeria. Although Azikiwe was a graduate of Howard University, another HBCU, he held close ties with Lincoln University. I discuss Azikiwe and Nkrumah in the chapter on Africa. Langston Hughes, one of Rev's closest friends, visited him occasionally. This was the era of the Harlem Renaissance, and Hughes was an important personality in that movement.

When I was about eleven or twelve, our fellowship group read and discussed the entire Bible. Rev called my mother seeking permission for me to join him and Langston Hughes during one of Hughes's visits. We three would discuss the issues of the day during lunch or dinner. I was familiar with Hughes's work from my reading of the *Tribune*, the *Pittsburgh Courier*, *Jet Magazine* (in later years), or other periodicals my mother purchased and brought home. Rev and I both knew many of his poems by heart. It was great fun to hear Hughes recite his own poems, as an example "I, Too":

> I, too sing America
> I am the darker brother.

I would counter with: "Mother to Son":

> Well, son, I'll tell you:
> Life for me ain't been no crystal stair.
> It's had tacks in it,
> And splinters,
> And boards torn up,

Poetry was an important part of our family. One of the women for whom my mother cleaned house discarded a book of poems by Henry Wadsworth Longfellow. My mother brought it home and we read a poem at the kitchen table every night after dinner. I still know many of Longfellow's poems by heart.

My mother also hosted teas as social gatherings for the Philadelphia chapter of the Alumni Association of Voorhees School and Junior College (now Voorhees University), where she served as president for many years. She invited Galilee church members, neighborhood friends, and others who loved poetry. Refreshments were the traditional homemade cake and nonalcoholic punch. Attendees recited their favorite poems. When I heard a poem I really liked, I asked the person reciting to write it down for me.

Learning these poems came in handy in later life when, as an advocate, activist, and ardent speaker for a specific cause, I wove in lines from appropriate poems into my presentations. Langston Hughes was impressed with my rather broad knowledge of poetry—especially by Black authors, including Paul Lawrence Dunbar, Gwendolyn Brooks, Maya Angelou, and James Weldom Johnson.

Rev was impressed too. I will never forget the BYPU weekly Wednesday evening meetings, often simply called fellowship. We all rushed to attend. I was obviously his most attentive student, always asking questions. We read the entire Bible three times during the years I attended Fellowship meetings. Yes, the entire Bible. I learned enough to challenge a Bryn Mawr professor's literary interpretation of several verses of Ecclesiastes. My knowledge of the Bible also came in handy when I debated Malcolm X many years later.

Not only did we read the Bible, but we also analyzed it under the Rev's supervision. There were in-depth discussions about Christ's early ministry, about differences among Protestant groups and between Catholicism and Protestantism. We analyzed Christ's Judaism and imagined what the phrase "King of the Jews" really meant—all buoyed by references from specific verses in the Bible.

We studied pictures of life and the times in the thirty years before Christ began teaching and imagined what working as a carpenter was like. Discussions about Christ's skin color and those of the disciples were illuminating. For example, Rev taught us that there were no portraits of Christ available before the fourth century AD. This is because all such portraits rendered him as Black. Given the location and climate of the Holy Land, it was only natural that Christ was Black. Rev introduced us to concepts of power, race, and discrimination, while explaining the scope of Christianity and the impact of Christ rendered as Black in that early era and since.

Our discussions about the meaning and significance of baptism were hot and heavy. I don't think Rev was at all surprised when I told my mother that I could not be baptized. We had a baptismal pool in the chancel that was perhaps four feet deep. It was initially constructed in the area where the choir, minister, and other service participants sat. Remember, too, that the church was built piecemeal because of limited funds.

I explained to my mother that I did not believe most of the basic principles of Christianity—much less the

Baptists. She demanded examples of what I didn't believe. I cited the virgin birth, Christ feeding the multitude with five loaves and three fishes, and the Resurrection and Ascension as examples. She replied that I should have faith and do it for her. Therefore, I was baptized.

I left home and Galilee to attend college and never fully returned. When I returned to Philadelphia to visit my family for holidays, we attended services at Galilee. I also returned for the passing of my mother and later my sister. I can only imagine the discussions Rev and I would have now about sexual abuse and racism in the church worldwide, much less Protestant evangelicalism and the church's declining membership. I noticed on a visit perhaps ten years ago that women are now permitted to serve as Trustees and Deacons. This was impossible during the time I attended church. Women did much of the work, but men controlled the church. This was true of Protestantism universally. Even today, I believe that there are few women in positions of power in the Catholic or Episcopal Church. Like Protestantism, both remain conservative and unwelcoming to women in formal leadership roles. Yet churches offer opportunities for women to hone leadership skills. These include organizing events, serving as main speakers at special occasions, and serving as Sunday School teachers. Women also lead at special ad hoc events.

Today Galilee has fewer than thirty-five members. Too many are elderly. Too many have limited financial resources for a host of reasons, with age the dominant factor. With so few members, the Church has difficulty paying its bills and maintaining its presence. The COVID pandemic adversely affected Galilee—like other churches—requiring Zoom services and limiting its pastoral work. These dwindling numbers also ring true with other churches in the neighborhood. The Roxborough Baptist Church has long closed. The Lutheran Church is an Imaging Center. Other denominations also face declining membership. The church as an institution is in big trouble when it comes to membership, credibility, influence, and power.

The retired Galilee minister, who was also president of the Black Clergy of Philadelphia, failed to maintain a steady church membership over thirty years, despite those who occasionally attended Galilee's services or lent their talents to rebuilding the church. There is now an interim minister. However, there is still a constituency for the church in the area. On a recent visit to the church to celebrate my younger brother's ninetieth birthday, I noticed two young White families participating in the event. I was told that they are members of the church. This is exciting for me because I have suggested that the church become interracial, and a number of young White families live in the community. Several young aspiring ministers have applied for the job as part-time ministers leading to full-time positions when finances improve. If Galilee is to survive, there must be real change in all areas of operation. I made suggestions to the remaining members. They will assess and respond as they see fit.

* * *

My resistance to baptism was and continues to be based on the belief that religion is a divisive force in our society. Intolerance, rather than tolerance, shapes daily actions. Wars result from demands that people embrace specific religions. Those who follow different religions are often ostracized or killed. People suffer, and lives are lost.

At eleven, I was not fully aware of religion's shortcomings. But I saw many who called themselves devout flout its principles repeatedly in their daily lives. As I grew older, I witnessed more of this. For example—treatment of the Jewish people, schisms in the church between and among various denominations, hostility between Muslims and Christians, and most recently the horrific outcome of the hostility between Israel and the Palestinians.

I did not come to my beliefs quickly. They emerged over time. I'm a "people watcher." I observe other people's actions, assess them, and ask myself, "Would you do that?" Almost always, the answer is "no" because the actions do not measure up to the high standards I set for myself.

As an example, in high school I asked the father of a good friend who had a thriving business to help me get a job. I needed the money to pay graduation expenses. He promised to do so. I kept reminding him. One day I realized that he was not going to help or hire me himself. He broke his word. I was very disappointed.

Another example: When Marvin and I were raising funds for CORE, a very wealthy friend offered to make a sizable contribution if I agreed to be his "secret" mistress. To be honest, I didn't know what a "secret mistress" was, but I knew instinctively that it was not a good thing. I refused. He did not contribute. CORE really needed the money. I felt, however, that my marriage vows and being crazy about my husband were more important than moncy. We would find it somewhere else, the right way. We did. I never mentioned this to Marvin.

I take pride in depending on myself. The very best way to motivate me is to tell me that I can't do something. If I can't—and it happens—I will seek help, but not before I exhaust every avenue trying to do it myself. Finally, let me say that I am not perfect. I made mistakes, sometimes big ones. I admit them, try very hard to learn from my mistakes and move on.

If you were to ask, "Is there a God in whom you believe?" I really don't know. I do know that there is someone or something out there helping me and looking out for me. I've come a long way. I am not a Christian. I am Every Woman who tries to live her life standing up for right and justice.

However, I do follow a faith. It is a belief in myself and others. A realization that when the chips are down most people will do the "right" thing—whatever that is. I follow the teachings in the Bible that I believe have merit: turn the other cheek, return evil with good, and love thy neighbor. I devoutly believe that I am, indeed, my brother's keeper. Those principles and others that my mother embraced guide my life.

8

A Negro at Bryn Mawr

As the only Negro resident student at Bryn Mawr College in 1950, believe me I was uncomfortable. Bryn Mawr was an elite Seven Sister Ivy League institution for White students. Three African American girls attended the college in the 1930s—including Enid Cook—but none were permitted to live on campus. An African American female accepted in 1946 lived on campus. I was therefore the second African American student to live on campus, but likely the first working-class Black resident student. African American girls followed me—many of whom had academic records which surpassed mine—but I paved the way, challenging established norms in the process.

White people are central to my earliest memories. We lived in an integrated community. Our next-door neighbor in Roxborough was White. At the elementary school I attended in West Philly all the teachers were White. So, too, when we returned to the Levering Elementary School in Roxborough. My siblings and I were the only Negro kids in the school. As noted above, Black youngsters who lived throughout Roxborough, Manayunk, and Wissahickon typically attended Joel Cook Elementary, which was closer geographically.

In both schools we practiced the principles stressed at home: "No one owes you anything! Respect your elders! Don't take things that do not belong to you! The teacher is king (queen). The teacher is *always* right!" And God forbid that there was a phone call home reporting an incident of disrespect toward a teacher. Out came the strap and a beating followed. There was no discussion or defense.

While obtaining good grades in most subjects, I was not artistic. Otherwise, I excelled. Roxborough High School (RHS) was similar to Levering Elementary. My mother insisted that we had to be twice as good as our peers to receive the credit we deserved. I participated in extracurricular activities, graduated, and was admitted to Bryn Mawr as a member of the Class of 1954 on a room, board, and tuition scholarship—a full ride. Bryn Mawr provided the tuition. Room and board were covered by the National Scholarship Service and the Fund for Negro

Students (NSSFNS). The latter, providing supplementary scholarships for Black students at interracial colleges in the United States, was administered by the National Student Association (NSA).

I was determined to live on campus rather than be a commuting (non-resident) student. Although Bryn Mawr is only twelve miles from Philadelphia, NSSFNS funds made that possible. In retrospect, I'm surprised by many of my college instincts. I knew that academics should be central to my experience, but equally important was living with girls my own age. I had a lot to learn from young women who—up until then—had a different lifestyle. Otherwise, I could have gone to Penn or Temple University. I also felt that I had much to gain from the larger Ivy League environment. I was right, of course. Life at Bryn Mawr was radically different from Roxborough.

Parents often ask me which college their youngster should select. I reply that while academics are extremely important, students can obtain a superb education at many schools. They do not have to be Ivies. Equally, if not more crucial, are the other young adults they will encounter. Shared experiences and lessons learned from one another make the difference. The possibility of forming lasting friendships through both work and at play is what really matters. The key question should be:

Does the school have a reputation for a positive growth experience?

I did not belong to a sorority. There were and still are no sororities at Bryn Mawr because they don't believe in them. Black sororities did not operate on campus, but in the larger community. I refused to join a Black sorority despite having been approached by two. Sororities are a given among the Black elite, but I do not consider myself a member of the Black elite.

I remember visiting Denbigh—my assigned residential hall—before school started and asking to see my room. Everyone had a single room, although wealthy girls shared suites between two connecting rooms. A graduate resident student (warden) presided over each dorm, tasked with looking out for us. In addition, the staff member in charge of housekeeping for the college lived in Denbigh. She told me that my name was not on the list when I visited. I insisted—primarily because I never had a room alone and was anxious to scope it out. She stood her ground, and I stood mine. Finally, she told me I was too uppity and that all the maids had signed in upon arrival. I told her I was *not* a maid. I was a student. She showed me my room.

From the very beginning everyone knew me since I was the only Black student on campus. I made a lot of friends, including girls who lived with me on the second floor. (Students majoring in German lived on the first floor.) We called dorms by their primary names, for example Rhoades rather than Rhoades Dormitory. Freshmen arrived from different parts of the country, but primarily from Mid-Atlantic states, the Midwest, and New England. They ran the gamut economically. Parent occupations ranged from Episcopalian bishop, to artist, psychiatrist, textile manufacturer, college professor, violinist in the New York Philharmonic, etc. Most were raised in well-to-do homes. The girls on my floor represented the student body in microcosm.

Wealthy students occasionally invited me to their homes for the weekend. I was amazed by their Park Avenue or Fifth Avenue family apartments. When the elevator opened, I discovered that their parents owned the entire floor. There were also girls like me from more modest backgrounds, but not nearly as modest as my own. Everyone was treated equally on campus—or so it seemed. We all ate the same food and went to the same classes. It wasn't until Friday morning before a trip home that students brought out their fur coats and leather luggage.

My Denbigh classmates taught me about the "bread and butter" letter: a thank-you note that must be sent after visiting someone's home. They taught me how to mix and match clothes to make it appear that I had a lot more than

I really did. They also taught me how to give myself a manicure and to play bridge. I taught them how to play pinochle. I stayed away from the few who were hostile. To this day some of my closest friends are Bryn Mawr alumnae.

I also made friends with upper-class students and some of the wealthier alumnae. In part it's because I was active politically from the beginning. We had a regional meeting of Students for Democratic Action (SDA) on campus. I invited the president of Bryn Mawr, Ms. McBride, to welcome us. I introduced her. This was my first encounter with Ms. McBride. Back then Bryn Mawr was a small school with about six hundred students. If you wanted to see the president, dean, or someone else in authority, all you had to do was to go to their office and make an appointment. Ms. McBride's assistant told me to put the invitation in writing—which I did.

Ms. McBride was surprised at my ability to move among the participants from the various local colleges and the ease with which I presented her to my peers. She came to another SDA campus gathering after that. Ms. McBride told me that she was pleased I invited her. Through the years she especially liked the way some of my older wealthy alum friends responded when I asked them for money for Bryn Mawr. I would make a persuasive case which—along with the actions of others—netted the college additional donations. Many years later I asked one of my accountant friends to add up the value of the total aid I received from the college including interest. It turns out I paid that money back many times over.

Once classes started, I threw myself into academic life. I liked my classes—some better than others. As one of the 32 percent of the class of 1954 who entered from public schools, I felt only partially prepared for the academic challenges I faced. They were mostly subtle. As an example, I thought the word "art" meant pictures hanging on the wall. I was surprised to encounter its various meanings and uses. For example, the term applies to those who have mastered the creative process within the various realms in which they work. Novelists are considered artists. Some college professors are considered artists. A sculptor or ballet dancer may be an artist.

The school I attended—Roxborough High School (RHS)—primarily served working-class students. Administrators hardly dared to imagine a student attending an "Ivy." To my knowledge, only one other RHS student followed me to Bryn Mawr, and she was White. I noticed immediately how my preparation failed to measure up to peers from the private schools and New York City's prestigious public schools like Hunter High School and the Bronx High School of Science.

In retrospect, my academic performance was above average although it was not stellar. As the only Negro student on the campus, I had to be "brilliant." Otherwise, why was I there? I always felt that such standards and expectations were unfair. My mother often told me that it is not where you came from but where you're going that counts. By this time, I knew that I wanted to be an activist, to address the disparities I saw all around me, and to join others in the continuing quest for the expansion of equity and equality. At graduation my grade point average was a smidgeon below 80, a barrier to graduating cum laude.

I wrote good research papers. Most of this I taught myself by asking friends who received higher grades to let me see their papers. Of course, I was delighted on those rare occasions when my classmates asked to see *my* paper. I analyzed the topics they chose, the structures they designed, the sources they cited, and the conclusions they reached. I read their footnotes with great interest. This came in very handy when I later served as Chair of the Employment Committee of New York CORE (Congress of Racial Equality).

CORE did a research project because the *Daily News*, New York City's largest tabloid, refused to hire Negroes except in very low-level jobs affording little opportunity for upward mobility. Undertaking a quick analysis of its overall practices, we were most incensed by the paper's insistence on publishing the race/ethnicity of those allegedly accused of wrongdoing. When they resisted our early efforts to change their policies, we picketed them as part of the negotiating process.

When that didn't work, we researched the owners in depth, learning a great deal about their business. Several of our White and Black members entered low-level jobs. We knew how many employees worked at the *Daily News*, where they worked, what they did, how much they were paid, what the newspaper's stock was selling for, how much money they made annually, etc. This knowledge and more shaped our "demands." We ultimately won that struggle. The *News* stopped including the race of those whom they reported as allegedly breaking the law. It also hired several of our members in a range of positions, including its first Negro reporter.

Bryn Mawr had a vibrant, extracurricular program. I was most impressed with the self-government or student government organization. Based on the notion that students were mature enough to govern themselves, it is best described by final examinations when there were *no* proctors. Students were expected to do the right thing—not to cheat or act in a way to compromise the examination process. So far as I know, it worked. I was also active in the Bryn Mawr League, designed to provide help and support to those who needed it. I was especially attracted to the league because I saw the leadership qualities exhibited by the chair, one of my classmates.

Simultaneously I remained active in the campus chapter of Americans for Democratic Action (ADA). I can't recall any special activities we did at school as part of ADA's student division (SDA), but I took the Paoli Local train into Philadelphia regularly where I joined College SDA buddies in various demonstrations. I scraped up train fare to get there on more than one occasion.

I also remember vividly the speeches of Patrick Murphy Malin, the Quaker pacifist, who set the standard for our various activities. Malin was close to Philadelphia ADA; the two organizations collaborated on a host of issues. Malin followed Roger Baldwin as Executive Director of the American Civil Liberties Union (ACLU), where he championed civil liberties for more than a decade—especially during the McCarthy era. A magnetic speaker, he championed civil liberties along with a host of progressive ideas and actions during the years that he led the ACLU.

My experiences at Bryn Mawr and my involvement in its various organizations prepared me for my life of advocacy and activism. I was one of the few females and the only Black involved in all of this. However, when we expanded our activities beyond the metropolitan Philadelphia and New York areas, Walter Carrington, our only other Black member attending Harvard Law School, joined us. The adult leaders of these movements did not treat us like children. They included us, listened to us, supported our involvement, and, on occasion, let us lead on an issue where we had recognizable expertise. The experience we gained was priceless, preparing us to take the lead in future years.

All of these activities, as well as early evening lectures I attended at the college, kept me very busy. Every time I saw an opportunity to learn or experience something new, I jumped at it. I remember lecture series, as well as contacts with visitors deemed outstanding, yet unknown to me. I attended everything and like a sponge absorbed all I could. Decades later I remember the Flexner Lecture Series and a visit by Bayard Rustin, the civil rights pacifist, whose philosophy intertwined with mine in strange ways years later as I initiated CORE activity. I met girls from all over the world, most of whom were friendly.

In my junior year I obtained a paid job as fire captain for Denbigh. It was my responsibility to schedule regular fire drills to ensure the safe evacuation of the dorm. I was supposed to notify the resident housekeeper in advance. Our resident housekeeper was the woman who assumed I was a maid during that initial visit my freshman year. I conveniently forgot to notify her in advance of several nighttime fire drills. She emerged wearing a long, white nightgown with a matching cap, similar to the illustrations in a Dickens or Eliot novel. The students laughed at her sleeping attire. She filed a complaint. I reapplied for the fire captain job in my senior year. I did not get it. I wonder why.

This housekeeper had her own bathroom. One night when I was confident that she would be in her bathroom preparing for bed, I entered her room—which was much larger than ours—and crawled under her bed. Near her bed was a rocking chair sitting on a small, beautiful area rug. I waited for her to go to sleep. When I was sure she was asleep, I began pulling the edge of the carpet. The rocking chair began to rock. She woke up, jumped up screaming and fled the "haunted" room. I made a hasty escape back to my room. Admittedly, I don't take pride in such antics today. Clearly, based on her experience, I could have been a maid. Her reaction was impersonal, but in retrospect my immature actions were personal. This is a cautionary tale. In retrospect, my thinking was flawed. An investigation followed, but they didn't suspect me.

I was close to the maids and porters who had their own space—an all-purpose room in the basement of the administrative building (Taylor Hall). They sewed beautiful curtains and a bedspread for my room—probably out of the best material they had available. I was unaccustomed to being waited on. It was a difficult adjustment for me.

I became fast friends with several maids and porters—particularly Pearl Edmonds and Louis White. They lived on the third floor of Denbigh. I would visit occasionally in the evenings to play pinochle. I was a good pinochle player, offering tips when they asked. They suggested that I *should not* work as a waitress in the Deanery—a fancy dining room on campus—because they did not want diners to think I was a maid. To the chagrin of an administrative staff member, I explored with my friends the benefits of organizing a union for the staff. It never happened.

Black at Bryn Mawr, an ongoing college project, focuses on the history of racism at Bryn Mawr. For example, I only recently learned that tunnels under the library were used exclusively by the Black servants of wealthy students in attendance. The idea was to hide their presence from the rest of the campus.

This should be no surprise. Linda Perkins's essay in the *Harvard Educational Review*, (Vol. 67, No.4; 1990), explains that Bryn Mawr was the last of the Seven Sisters to admit women students of color. She attributes this partly to its location as the southernmost "female Ivy." During past years Bryn Mawr has been challenged over issues of diversity, the names on the various buildings, and much more. So, too, have other colleges and universities including the Ivies. As an aside, let me note that there were instances of antisemitism at the college as well, fueled by one of its earliest founders, M. Carey Thomas, who was ardently opposed to the admission of Jewish students as well as Negro students.

Don't Forget to Remember (Me) is a monument to the unexamined histories of Black students and staffers at the college. Designed by artist Nekisha Durrett, the work appears in a public plaza, with some 250 terra-cotta pavers engraved with the names of alums who blazed a trail at the school, as well as administrators who made the college function. Two Bryn Mawr students initiated this project in 2015 as part of their independent study work, and other projects have since emerged which amplify it.

I decided to attend Bryn Mawr because it figured into my ambitions of living a different kind of life from my parents, relatives, siblings, and childhood friends. Participation in student activities beyond campus was key and ultimately shaped my future life. A highlight was my attendance at Ohio State University at the annual meeting of the National Student Association (NSA) in 1954.

I was active throughout my years at college with Students for Democratic Action (SDA), the student affiliate of Americans for Democratic Action. Through SDA I met and became friends with peers at a host of nearby schools including Swarthmore, the University of Pennsylvania, and Temple University. Through membership in the Regional NSA organization, I met students from Cornell, City College of New York, Sarah Lawrence, and other colleges and universities.

Ultimately, the regional group chose to affiliate with the Young Adult Council (YAC). Membership included national youth groups such as: Young Christian Workers Collegiate Council for the United Nations and National Association of Colored People (NAACP) Youth Councils. YAC was sponsored by and operated under the aegis of the National Social Welfare Assembly. YAC was also the US representative on the Coordinating Secretariat of the National Union of Students (COSEC), the counterpart of the Communist-dominated International Union of Students (IUS).

In this environment many events occurred. During my senior year at Bryn Mawr (1954), I had a date with a Negro male. We went to The Greeks, a local restaurant that I patronized throughout my college career. We were denied service. When I questioned the owner, he admitted that he knew me and his restaurant served me in the past but noted that he did not "serve Negroes in groups." When I told my classmates what happened, they insisted that I tell Ms. McBride. This resulted in a suit brought on my behalf by Bryn Mawr College against the restaurant.

The college argued that if it had admitted me, it had a responsibility to make available all the opportunities and experiences other students enjoyed. The entire campus rallied to my support.

Just before the court case was to begin, the restaurant owner capitulated and rescinded the policy. The college then decided that all restaurants should follow The Greeks. Subsequently, Bryn Mawr students, joined by students from Haverford (a nearby male college), tested most of the restaurants on the Main Line of Philadelphia to ensure access to everyone. The word went out and, indeed, we were served everywhere. My life as an activist had begun. I realized that I was not alone in this endeavor. I owe Bryn Mawr College for launching me on a mission that has driven my activities, directly or indirectly, ever since.

When I was on the verge of graduation in 1954, the Cold War between the United States and the Soviet Union was at its height. I was selected to be a member of a US youth delegation associated with the founding of NATO—the North Atlantic Treaty Organization, which represented democratic nations, as opposed to the Warsaw Pact which represented communist nations. The two competing youth groups—COSEC and IUS—met periodically in bi-annual conferences to play out the conflicts between the US and the Soviet Union. The World

Assembly of Youth (WAY) was formed in this period, hosting meetings bringing together representatives from both COSEC and the IUS.

I continued my interest and involvement in international affairs from a youth perspective after graduation as the Executive Director of ADA's Student Group. In 1956 I attended a WAY meeting in Berlin, subsequently traveling throughout West Germany with young people from colonial territories in French-speaking Africa. This was my first contact with young men who would become emerging leaders for independence within colonial territories in Africa. I subsequently chaired the US Delegation to the 1958 meeting of WAY in New Delhi, India, in 1958.

In 1960, many of the colonial countries which my African friends represented became independent. Some became ambassadors to the United States and/or chief delegates to the United Nations. Our friendships continued into the future. I returned home with the experience with The Greeks coupled with attendance at international conferences abroad ready to take on new challenges and opportunities.

Seventy years after graduation I am still frequently asked to identify the most important thing I learned at Bryn Mawr. Questioners are disappointed when I tell them that it was the exposure to the White power structure, the opportunity to learn what it is, how it works and how to deal with it. (There is also a Black power structure that in many ways resembles the White power structure.) The White power structure is invisible. It also is everywhere. However, its expressions are both tangible and intangible. Those most affected by it can feel it most of the time.

Founded on lies in the areas of race, sex, and social class, those with power operate and benefit from it. Those without power nevertheless accept and adapt to it. It is inextricably linked with White culture. Women carry the culture even though it is a White male power structure that they are supporting, teaching, and expressing. Babies encounter it at birth. Young tots express it even at play; then preschool; then kindergarten through high school and finally adulthood.

At Bryn Mawr I observed it in the subtle way staff interacted with maids and porters, professors interacted with less advantaged students, and administrators interacted with faculty. Of course, it was not explicit nor widely practiced. An example is the student from somewhere in the South who complained to the warden about the presence of another African American student at meals. She wanted the warden to exclude the student from joining her fellow classmates at mealtimes. The warden refused and told the student that she could exclude herself, but the African American student would not be excluded.

Ralph Ellison describes the White power structure in *The Invisible Man.* Ellison's Invisible Man is invisible because no one can see him. They can't see beyond his skin color. I would add sex and social class as fundamental components of the White power structure. For me, White power describes one's actions in an environment supportive of White power—which is most environments—and the ability to use race, sex, and social class to the detriment of another person. People of color encounter instances of prejudice and discrimination on a regular basis. Black women have encountered the White power structure since time memorial. It is true that women have made gains in many areas of life, but the raw fact remains that we are second-class citizens in US society and many men resent the gains achieved thus far.

Peggy McIntosh describes manifestations and examples of White privilege and the White power structure in action in her essay, *White Privilege: Unpacking the Invisible Knapsack.* For me the most telling expression is the assertion that many White people are unaware of the privileges they enjoy simply by being White. This is only partially true, I believe, because today's environment and actions illustrate an awareness by Whites that their power is being diminished—perhaps even eroded.

Other examples McIntosh proposes include easier access to housing and expanded job opportunities. This, however, is the world people of color live in. We can sit back, accept and support it, or fight back.

I will not describe the instances of prejudice and discrimination I faced because of skin color or social class. There were and are many. I decided long ago to be a player rather than a victim, to lead the way rather than to complain, and to expand opportunities for all of us. Bryn Mawr played a special role in helping me on this mission.

* * *

At my public high school graduation in 1950 I received a copy of Edith Finch's *Carey Thomas of Bryn Mawr.* I still have it. The book chronicles Thomas's struggle for the higher education of women. Seventy years later, I insist that we tell her story and others that resonate with us. We must retell them over and over again to all who might/will listen. Today's youth have little idea of the struggles we endured over the years. We must share stories of struggle and oppression that bring women to where we are today—still struggling and still oppressed.

1. A popular slogan when I was in school: "Black is beautiful." But Black is not beautiful because of our past. It is beautiful because we are. I am me because I

am Black. But blackness is my Black experience, not my genes. Indeed, what really lies beyond slogans?

2. Today I join my aged, Black, Brown, and White sisters—supported by the National Mobilization Against Sweatshops—in chanting their slogan, "No More 24!" The slogan symbolizes their struggle against a New York State statute, A3415A—enforced only in New York City—requiring older home attendants to work twenty-four-hour shifts, sometimes two shifts consecutively, caring for Medicaid patients. They are paid for only thirteen hours per twenty-four-hour shift. These aged home attendants have resisted, using legal services, demonstrations, picket lines and, most recently, a hunger strike. This work endangers their health and their lives. Yet, this oppression of the powerless continues. Use of my slogan and theirs represents a mandate to challenge injustice encountered everywhere and to change the world we never made.

3. Bryn Mawr helped me develop the tools I use to hasten the changes I feel must come. I refuse to be intimidated by anyone Black or White. I have processed hair and an unprocessed mind. I refuse to accept the yoke of conformity—whether it comes from Blacks or Whites. I will think and live my own ideas. I will continue to accept people for what they are and my country for its possibilities. I accept the responsibility to translate those possibilities into performance and in my lifetime.

4. I see my Class of 1954 as a metaphor for my endearing and continuing relationships with Bryn Mawr women: Barbara Thatcher, Frieda Wagoner, Claire Liachowitz, Nancy Hayward, Molly Plunkett, Chloe Drabkin, Marion Pertz, Barbara Kalb, Jane Miller, Helen Thurston, Dianne Johnson, Ryna Appleton, Joyce Mitchell, Luvon Roberson, Nia Turner, and so many others. We shared adventures, many intangible and continuing.

5. I see activism as a key component of the Bryn Mawr experience. My activism, spawned in an African American working-class family, found its voice on campus and beyond. My tolerance, acceptance, and ultimately respect for those holding different views grew. Activism shaped my life and continues to do so today.

6. Bryn Mawr builds leaders. There are different kinds of leaders, some recognized and others not. The price of leadership is steep. I remind myself repeatedly that all too often you win when you lose; that in defeat you retreat and prepare to fight yet again. I am intrigued by today's responses to adversity, especially on the part of young women of color who are justifiably critical of the flaws in society but seek a "safe space" and anonymity rather than standing/fighting publicly. You never win that way.

7. Finally, growing old is my newest adventure. Organizing seniors to stand and fight in the midst of

trying times exacerbated by the pandemic gives me renewed energy. Finding new, creative ways to stay alive, in touch, while in the struggle is a challenge. I do so through my leadership in progressive organizations, my "group of buddies," and my newsletters. Taking my message far and wide, I'm reminded of my mother's words, "Always stand up for right and justice. When you do, never look around!"

9

Making It Happen: Turning a High School Around

Some say that the High School Division of the New York City Board of Education set me up when I was appointed principal of Andrew Jackson High School in August 1980. Others say I was naïve to take the job, to believe that I could make a difference while lacking administrative experience inside the system. Still others recognized that the chancellor sought change and took a calculated risk. Some thirty months later, sod covered the athletic field at Jackson, where dirt previously symbolized a high school marked for abandonment.

Jackson in August 1980 was indisputably the most difficult school in Queens. Inside walls were covered by graffiti. Beer and whiskey bottles blotted the grounds and periphery. Several buildings across the street were empty. The police no longer responded to calls for assistance. Large numbers of students spent the day in the halls. The cafeteria was a haven for drug peddlers. Certain stairways were declared off-limits for staff and students. An atmosphere of fear permeated the building. At the beginning of each new term, parents pressured the superintendent to transfer their children to other Queens high schools. Staff picketed the superintendent, demanding increased security. Newly assigned teachers and staff often refused to appear.

A little more than two years later, not only was grass growing on the athletic field, but hope and expectation for the school's future were evident among students, staff, and the community. Inside, the building was clean. Most of the 3,050 minority students walked to classes in an orderly fashion. Many carried books. Instructional supervisors gained credibility. Cafeteria and custodial staff resonated with pride and achievement. Secretaries and para-professionals were convinced the school could succeed—as were community residents who previously refused to send their children.

At the first faculty conference in September 1980, I shared my goals for the year: change the school's public image; improve basic skills; expand career and occupational programs; and establish minimal standards.

While ambitious benchmarks, a new framework was imperative. My unstated targets: create an administrative structure; introduce discipline; and build a creative educational environment. I absorbed case studies about change and leadership at the Harvard Business School, where my own child was enrolled. Instinctively, I knew that Harvard's tried and tested management procedures must be adapted for Jackson, where Black kids—mostly working class and underachievers—had all but given up. The school required a leader, and I was on stage.

In a sense, my background prepared me for the assignment. As the first working-class Black student to enter Bryn Mawr College as an undergraduate in 1950, I understood what it was like to be alone, misunderstood, and the object of unreasonable expectations. Surviving that experience, I worked hard, fought back from defeat, and learned how to operate within the system. I also gained an understanding of power—how it is used and abused.

I was a visible principal, constantly in the halls talking with the students who should have been in class. I saw the problems firsthand in a way both experienced and casual observers cannot understand. Many students arrived late. Some did not come to school at all. Others came into the building but did not go to their homeroom or to class. Fortunately, a core group attended class to learn.

General school discipline was a formidable challenge. Before the school year opened, I met with the Cabinet of Assistant Principals to develop a discipline program. We set standards for appropriate behavior and provided written rules for students on the first day of school. Violators were disciplined. Much time was spent conducting conferences with students and parents to discuss problems, identify options and propose/implement appropriate solutions. These included a return to class, transfer to another school, or after-school counseling or other support. More than 170 conferences were held in 1980–81, with a slightly smaller number the following year.

Unfortunately, the discipline issue did not apply solely to students. Staff presented their own problems, ranging from failure to observe basic rules, such as arriving on time, refusing to punch in or out, and poor classroom management routines that stymied education. Most teachers did not stand outside their doors during class changes, offering a myriad of excuses for failing to do so. A number of staff applauded my rule-obeying efforts for students, but refused to do the same.

Student achievement was a major thorn. More than half were two or more years below grade level in reading. Almost two thirds were two or more years below grade level in mathematics. About 40 percent of the ninth grade were holdovers, with some as old as eighteen or nineteen.

Shunted aside into homogeneously grouped classes, little was expected of them; failure to achieve was woven into their school career. Unfortunately, too many teachers had given up, concluding these children could not learn. Teachers also lacked supervision, staff development programs, books and other basic tools, plus a willingness to promote change. Visits to our feeder junior high schools confirmed my view that elementary and intermediate level schools in our area were failing students.

Walking the halls, I recognized a compelling need for recognition and respect. Students often lived in foster homes with large numbers of foster brothers and sisters. For others, the only decent meals they received were served in our school cafeteria at breakfast and lunch. There was also little to do after school. In retrospect, I spent too much of my time disciplining students and too little time working with them, guiding them, getting to know them. However, from my first day, I referred to students and staff by his/her title and last name. They were surprised by "Mr., Mrs. or Ms.," although they called me Dr. Rich. Doing so set a professionalism standard. Custodial workers and para-professionals also serve an important role. Because I worked menial jobs, I appreciated their need for recognition and respect.

While teachers wanted to succeed, there was deep room for improvement. For example, insisting on security and safety, staff thought security guards should protect them. Yet, well-planned and executed lesson plans were/are the best disciplinary tool. Against this background, I spent the 1980–81 academic year bringing structure and discipline to the school. By June, change was visible in cleaner halls, improved attendance, and better administrative procedures. Slowly the school began to change.

Working together, staff produced a manual on administrative and safety procedures. Representatives from business and industry, including the 100 Black Men and the Coalition of 100 Black Women, visited classes to share specific vocations. Science students won first prize in a boroughwide science research contest for a group project. Latin was introduced, as well as a new course in probability for low achievers. New security guards replaced less effective ones, and an intrusion alarm system was installed. Students collaborated with the dietitian to ensure menus reflected their tastes. Programs in business and health careers—funded via the New York City Board of Education Target Schools Project—were offered. A computerized system to monitor attendance was introduced. The Parents' Association increased its involvement and impact in the school.

My goal for the 1981–82 school year was student retention and achievement advances. My unstated goal: building a constituency for the school and increasing student involvement in Jackson. A new custodian engineer and staff transformed the building over the summer. Brass bannisters in the entrance hall shone. The first floor and stairwells were painted. Maintenance of the area around the school improved markedly. Students who violated reasonable rules and regulations knew they would be disciplined. The influx of new students, however, continued poor achievement patterns. Suspension conferences declined, but only slightly. I continued to monitor halls and stairwells during classes. Word gradually went out that Jackson's new principal meant business.

Actions against drug peddlers made it increasingly difficult to buy drugs near or inside the school. The scent of marijuana could still be found in an occasional stairway, but pity the perpetrator discovered by the principal or staff member. Guns, knives, and improvised weapons diminished. Formal and informal conferences with the security guards improved performance and raised morale. Stricter enforcement of our identification card system made it more difficult for trespassers to enter the building.

My 1980 visit to the precinct commander appealing for enhanced security was unsuccessful. I hoped to speak with him about assigning an officer to the school. He told me no, he didn't want to discuss it. He didn't provide a reason. I was completely unaware that a policeman was assigned to our school because he was hiding in the furnace room.

They wouldn't even speak with me. So early one morning in the fall of 1981, I visited the precinct to discuss changes we made, highlighting my commitment to discipline, hard work, and achievement. To my delight, two officers volunteered to work in the area adjacent to the school, beginning a relationship with Jackson that continues to this day. The continuous presence of uniformed police officers brought safety to the building and nearby community. Our computerized system monitoring attendance gradually extended to those arriving late and/or cutting classes. We informed parents at an early stage. Although cutting and lateness were still at unacceptable levels, they improved.

My increased observation schedule played a significant role in improving instruction. A policy of unannounced visits to classrooms was implemented. Post-observation conferences with teachers highlighted ways instruction could be improved. Visits from borough chiefs in physical education, remedial English, mathematics, and social studies provided additional substance to the academic programs. Student performance in the Science Department improved, largely due to a newly assigned chairperson mobilizing his staff. Introduction of a new computer science course tapped the interest of students, along with courses in Basic and Pascal programming languages. Strengthened vocational courses also had a positive impact on students. Automobile mechanics and general contracting courses supplemented our business education, health careers, and fashion programs.

Student support grew during 1981–82. Student participation in the Consultative Council for parents and community representatives was important. The New York *Daily News* ran a story about our Youth Outreach Unit (YOU) program, linking plainclothes police with teachers in self-awareness sessions for ninth-year students. The Official Class Forum, an outgrowth of YOU, offered students a vehicle for expressing concerns. Efforts to reach the community accelerated during the second year. Our marching band performed at many civic functions in Queens and throughout New York City. Mixed and Gospel Choruses sang at senior citizens' centers, winning prizes in choral competitions Producing the first play in many years, students received schoolwide and community acclaim for *A Raisin in the Sun*.

A homecoming event in the winter of 1983 mobilized alumni and community members in a series of activities, including a parade, a football game, and a ball, which became the talk of the neighborhood. We established contact with the Cambria Heights Civic Association, the Cambria Heights Sports Association, block associations around the school, as well as various religious and civil associations. A camera and film for identification cards provided by a local bank improved security and discipline. Friends of Jackson brought in key people from the neighborhood and beyond to rebuild the school. Liaison with the Coalition of 100 Black Women also helped in many ways.

Midway into my third year as principal, I reviewed changes that occurred at Jackson. Performance on reading and mathematics standardized tests improved. Regents Competency Test (RCT) scores measuring basic skills improved. There were also modest gains on Regents exams in academic areas, despite increases in the number of students taking these tests. Test performance by pupils with special educational needs increased in the ninth, tenth, and eleventh grades, while students in the twelfth grades maintained their performance levels.

Equally important, however, was the good feeling larger numbers of students and staff conveyed about their school. Instruction improved, with staff development programs for teachers in place. Jackson was a different school. Acceptance of change is not easy. The public had not yet caught the new spirit, but changes were an open secret in Queens and beyond.

Much credit belongs to supervisors and teachers, secretaries, para-professionals, cafeteria, security, and custodial workers who helped by doing their jobs well, and then doing more. Their number grew daily. Fellow principals responded graciously to my requests for assistance. Credit also belongs to a small group of personal friends who provided a small discretionary fund for instructional items and extracurricular programs.

Without Chancellor Frank Macchiarola, however, I would not have been selected as principal. With a PhD in African Studies and Education, I like to believe he chose me because I could do the job, rather than because I was Black and female. I believe he shared my view that public schools can nurture excellence; that all children, including Black youth, deserve the best.

10

Tough Love: Highlights at Andrew Jackson High School (1980–1985)

Yes, I likely broke the law, but it was worth it. Tough love works. Structural racism permeates American society. Nowhere was it more evident than in Andrew Jackson High School in the 1980s. This southeast Queens school is located near the Nassau County border. Nassau is one of two counties on Long Island; the other is Suffolk County. These two, along with parts of Brooklyn and Queens, constitute Long Island. Only Queens—occupying the western section of Long Island—is part of New York City.

Recent studies highlight segregated housing patterns in NYC, as illustrated by the Queens borough. Very few African Americans live in Nassau and Suffolk, the wealthier counties. Imagine 1980, when even fewer, if any, African Americans lived in these areas. The majority of White teachers at Andrew Jackson High School resided in Nassau County. Teaching at Jackson was attractive because of geographical proximity to their homes. Jackson support staff was primarily African American and lived in Queens. This was the backdrop for my first "tough love" effort.

An English teacher reported three students for turning his car upside down—a Volkswagen, a very small car. The teacher identified the perpetrators. Surprised, I suggested that we meet, along with his United Federation of Teachers (UFT) chapter representative and the allegedly guilty students. We held a conference in my office that afternoon—the teacher, his three students, and the UFT chapter chair. When I informed the threesome of the teacher's accusation, they admitted the act—claiming they took revenge because he was failing them as a teacher. Dumbfounded, I instructed them to turn his car right side up and watched while they did so.

At 8:00 the next morning, this teacher's first class of the day, I stood outside his classroom door. He was late. I then observed his class and was underwhelmed. I asked,

"May I see your lesson plan?" He didn't have one. (The UFT was in discussions with the Board of Education about the efficacy of lesson plans. The union insisted that they were unnecessary.) I told him, "We will have a post-observation conference today during your free period. I suggest you bring the chapter chairman with you."

I said his lesson was unsatisfactory. Developmental building blocks—the bedrock of NYC public schools—were missing. Further, the teacher had no alternative lesson plan. For example: I asked why he called on only four students. There were about twenty-three or so present. He told me that he tried in the past, but they didn't answer. I later showed him how to get all students present to answer by addressing each one individually.

The very next morning, I waited outside his first period classroom again. The teacher was late again. Several days later, I presented him with a written report of our post-observation conference and the lesson I observed. The teacher filed a Board of Education grievance report against me, reviewed by the superintendent, the Central Board of Education, and a designated arbitrator. At each step, my determination of his lesson as unsatisfactory was sustained.

The long-term result was that the teacher received an unsatisfactory rating for the school year, based on attendance and performance. However, from then on he prepared his lessons more carefully. Students never turned his car upside down again.

I discovered that the absence of textbooks was a major impediment to a vibrant, valid instructional program. Procedures for returning textbooks were not fully honored by the students. The result: I did not have enough textbooks to distribute to students on almost every subject. I needed a way to convince students to bring books back to school at the end of the semester. After numerous requests, which resulted in very few textbooks being returned, I decided that a more creative plan was needed.

This was 1980, and the beginning of the so-called "Rap" movement. A form of music I do not fully understand to this day, it appealed to my students. I discovered that a famous Rap group, Run-DMC, lived in southeast Queens, where the school was located. (AJHS was in Cambria Heights. Other nearby areas were Hollis, St. Albans, and the more distant South Jamaica.) I sent word to its three members—Joseph Simmons (Run), Jason Mizell (Jam Master Jay), and Darryl McDaniels (DMC)—asking to meet, and they appeared. I explained my challenge and asked them to perform a series of concerts in the school auditorium. The price of admission to their concert was a textbook. Or, for students who did not have a textbook at home, five dollars. Run-DMC agreed. I then went to the Art Department Chair and requested that the art classes create posters announcing the concert, to be placed around the school. (I still have a poster.) I invited reporters from local Queens papers to write about the concerts.

On the designated day, I had three concerts, back-to-back, in the school auditorium, which held about eight hundred students. I collected hundreds of books for my instructional program. The concerts were a great success. I told the Run-DMC performers how indebted I was to them for this boost to the instructional program. Students began to realize that I was on their side; that I was working for them. Not all of them believed it, but the number gradually grew. The reporters did a wonderful job, which created great press for our school and the group. Run-DMC went on to become very famous. Sadly, Jason Mizell was murdered around 2000. The police have recently solved his murder, explaining it as a cocaine deal that had gone wrong. Joseph Simmons, brother of the rap mogul Russell Simmons, went on to become the well-known Pentecostal minister, Reverend Run.

* * *

William Fulbright was a famous Senator from Arkansas in the United States Congress. In 1945, he introduced and received approval of legislation codifying the Fulbright program. This was a scholar exchange program between the United States and European countries torn apart during World War II. The funds generated from the sale of surplus World War II equipment provided the bedrock funding for the Fulbright program. The program was an exchange program where young scholars from the United States could study at universities in European countries and scholars from those countries could study in the United States. It exists to the present day and is perhaps today's most prestigious scholarly exchange program.

When I first went to Andrew Jackson High School, I had some angry, destructive students enrolled in my school. I was required to suspend many for fighting, drug dealing, being verbally abusive to the staff, even setting fire to the school. Many teachers were afraid of them. These students were unsuccessful in school. Some, at eighteen or nineteen years old, were still in the ninth grade.

According to the Board of Education guidelines, I could suspend students for up to five days. Guidance counselors call the parents of suspended students. We would have a conference. Too many parents admitted that they had given up on their child and did not know what to do. All too frequently, according to the rules of the Board of Education, I was required to bring the students back into school after this conference. However, these students were so out of control, I really felt that I could not do that. So, I devised "The Andrew Jackson High School Fulbright Program."

This is how it worked. There were perhaps sixteen Queens high schools. I was on friendlier terms with some of their principals more than others. In preparation for these conferences, I would call up a friendly principal and say, "John, you are truly lucky because you are being invited to participate in the Andrew Jackson High School Fulbright program. This program is an exchange program. I am awarding a Fulbright to a particular student, so that he can attend your school. In return for accepting this student from the Andrew Jackson High School Fulbright program, I will take one of your suspended students who you deem would thrive much better in an environment where he or she knows no other students. I will accept him/her into the Andrew Jackson High School Fulbright program at Jackson."

Over the course of several years, I placed very troubled students who could not thrive and function effectively at Jackson in other Queens high schools. Principals knew me from my work with the Queens superintendent and understood how troubled Jackson was. Some laughed at my appointment behind my back, insisting that I would never survive there. But twelve principals, mostly male, helped me out. Several who took a student told their colleagues and soon other principals were willing to take students. It's called "moral suasion."

If I could not find a principal willing to take a student, I placed him/her in a small business job near the school. There were dry cleaners, supermarkets, stationery stores, and other kinds of small business enterprises. I would approach owners and say, "I have a student for you. This student will come to work every day from nine a.m. until three p.m., and you will teach the student your business. I will visit periodically to meet with you and the student to assess their performance. We will then determine whether the student can come back to school."

Placing students in businesses around the school required parental permission. I also explained to the student and their parents that they were not yet ready to come back to my school. They had to show me that their behavior had changed in a way in which they could now join this newly created environment that prevailed at Jackson. Now, all of this was likely against education practices of the time, but the parents almost always agreed.

Admittedly, there was some crime in the neighborhood around the school. An interesting by-product of this "addendum" to the Andrew Jackson High School Fulbright Program is that no enterprise in which we placed a Jackson student was ever robbed. Student participants came to know the area's residents. Their behaviors often changed for the better. We were able to return them to school with a new attitude and new motivation.

Word went out that this principal (me) really meant business. Nevertheless, there were students at Andrew Jackson High School who most of the teachers, support staff, and students feared. I could not let these students return to school, I could not put them into my Fulbright program, nor could I put them in the addendum to the Fulbright program. For these students, I created "Operation Excellence."

I wasn't afraid of these students, and they knew it. Over the years I had dealt with many "bad" kids. These were no different except that I had a chance to help them. They somehow suspected that I was trying to help.

I had a very good friend whose name was Jo List Levinson. Jo was very wealthy. She provided me with a modest fund for Operation Excellence. Jo also had a friend, Meyer Parodneck, who ran an organization called the Consumer Farmer Cooperative (which became the Parodneck Foundation when he passed away). The Consumer Farmer Cooperative made grants and low- or no-cost loans to fight deplorable housing conditions throughout New York City.

Jo helped me purchase an abandoned house from the United States Department of Housing & Urban Development (HUD). The house was very inexpensive, maybe two or three thousand dollars. It was located in southeast Queens, near the school. The Consumer Farmer Cooperative also had relationships with the Cambria Heights Civic Association. This association's members included craftsmen (plumbers, electricians, carpenters, landscape developers, painters, wallpaper hangers, etc.). I met with them, explaining that I had students who were not successful in school—that I wanted them to learn a trade and needed their help with Operation Excellence.

Students I could not take back into the school were placed in Operation Excellence—rehabilitation of the abandoned house. First, they worked with a plumber. The plumber, who was a member of the Cambria Heights Civic Association, taught them how to install and maintain the plumbing system—everything they needed to know about being a plumber. Then I had a carpenter do the same thing. The money Jo List Levinson gave me bought the supplies we used to renovate the home.

The skilled craftsmen supervised, but it was the students who renovated the house. It took several years to rehabilitate this house because it was in shambles when we purchased it. Individual students cycled through the program. Periodically, I visited students working on jobs in the community. Then I visited students rehabbing the house. The students reported to work every day from 9:00 a.m. to 3:00 p.m., just as if they were going to school. I said to them, "If I come to visit, and you're not here, I will see to it that you are never absent again."

They were afraid of me. I never told them what I was going to do. All I would say is that I would "act appropriately." I visited regularly. Over the course of several years, students worked on the house. Once they finished rehabilitating it, we held a press conference. I invited television stations and newspapers to come. Students gave a presentation, showing television audiences all the work they had done. Following our press conference, I allowed these students to return to school. We held a raffle to sell the house, which raised $20,000 because the house was really very attractive when the students finished rehabilitating it.

Then we bought another house and started all over again. Operation Excellence remained in place during my years at Jackson.

* * *

The school was not all "bad." I had some terrific kids in the school. Andrew Jackson was a magnet school in music and in art. As noted, I reached out to the art department to design posters for the rap concert. I also reached out to the music department. The music program was not highly developed when I arrived. People tend to assume that Black kids are innately musically talented. I think it's a myth, but they are musically inclined. One of the things that we did early on was resuscitate the Andrew Jackson High School Gospel Chorus. Let me tell you, these kids could sing. We would have free concerts at night, invite the community, show off the Gospel Chorus and offer refreshments after the concert. I asked teachers to bake cakes and pies. I baked cakes. We had coffee, cake, brownies, and soda as refreshments.

I wanted to promote good feelings about the school. The school's colors were green and white. I therefore required that every youngster wear green gym shorts and a white tee shirt during gym class, which they soon did. I also directed students to paint the athletic field bleachers. On the big wall behind the bleachers, they painted in green and white the school's slogan, WE CAN BECAUSE WE KNOW WE CAN.

At the end of my first year, parents requested creation of the Andrew Jackson High School Marching Band. I thought that was a great idea. However, we needed an orchestral music teacher and instruments. So, I put my feelers out and learned that a New York City high school with an orchestral music program was closing. Barry Domfort was the music teacher there. I invited him to come to Andrew Jackson as our orchestral music teacher. He accepted my invitation. Mr. Domfort was able—I don't know how—to requisition the instruments from the school that was closing. We put the word out in the community, using posters and other mechanisms, that we were forming the Andrew Jackson High School Marching Band. We programmed classes so kids in the band could attend music class together. Mr. Domfort's gift, in my view, was his ability to motivate students. By the end of the first semester, the band was really quite good.

Next, I went to the Parents' Association and told them, "You know, the band needs uniforms." With some of the money from the Principal's Fund, we bought material; the parents in the Parents' Association sewed green and white uniforms for the band. The band started performing at football games, because we had a football team. They were wonderful.

I guess it was early March of my second year at the school when the New York City Fire Department approached me and asked me if the Andrew Jackson High School Marching Band could lead the fire department up Fifth Avenue in the annual St. Patrick's Day parade. The Fire Department, many years later, still does not have a reputation of being responsive to Blacks. Yet, the Andrew Jackson High School Marching Band, for many years afterward, was the marching band for the New York City Fire Department.

One final example of good things at AJHS: Mrs. Barbara Clark—the Parents' Association president who later served as the assemblywoman for Southeast Queens and is now deceased—organized a Homecoming. The idea was that alumni would return for a weekend, and there would be a series of events celebrating the school. Homecoming became a big event at Jackson. I'm not sure when it began, but certainly by the fall of my second or third year. Homecoming events involved a Gospel Chorus concert, the football game with the marching band, and then a cookout on the athletic field. Our athletic field was substantial because the school took up an entire city block.

We had a significant Haitian population in the school. During one of the Homecoming events, the Haitian parents built a fire on the field in a designated area and roasted a goat. Other parents grilled frankfurters and hamburgers. We had soft drinks, and parents brought cakes. We had athletic events like relays. Students and alums especially looked forward to the evening dance in the beautifully decorated gym. All these positive opportunities—the Gospel Chorus, marching band,

and Homecoming—brought character, meaning, and a hopeful spirit to our youth, teachers, employees, and the larger community.

11

Challenges and Opportunities

Students, teachers, and people in the community laughed when they saw my size: five foot two inches, 110 pounds. Few believed I could exert control over Jackson. Yet, by the end of my second year, even the toughest students and most cynical teachers were afraid of me. I began the job with a reprimand from the New York City Board of Education, but even that didn't stop me. There are no *problems*—only *challenges and opportunities.*

The New York City Board of Education uses the file letter as a major disciplinary tool. I received my first (of several) file letters early on as principal of Andrew Jackson High School. Although not the faculty's choice, I was appointed in late June of 1980 and met with all the assistant principals in a friendly introductory session. Students had already dispersed for the summer. As soon as the school year started, I was declared in violation for failing to immunize 1,500 students. How was that possible?

Permit me to back up. Becoming a principal was the next step in my professional career in the New York City public school system. I began as a social studies teacher in 1962 in a middle school in Astoria, Queens, then transferred to the John Bowne High School in Flushing, Queens, in 1965. I taught at Far Rockaway High School following a leave of absence from 1971–76. During the intervening years, I completed course work for my PhD and directed the School Services Division of the African American Institute.

As noted in an earlier chapter, I became a teacher because a school was located across the street from Marvie's and my co-op apartment, and we needed additional income. As the Community Relations Director of the Congress of Racial Equality (CORE), Marvin was deeply involved in the Civil Rights Movement. In 1962, CORE was in the midst of the "Freedom Rides," an effort to end discrimination in interstate travel across the United States. The riders were traveling throughout the South; there were many, all employed by or closely allied with CORE. Marvin came home on several paydays with bad news. "We're not getting paid because CORE doesn't have any money."

It was his job to raise the money. He would say, "We have so many freedom riders in jail and countless field workers in numerous states. But we have limited funds and must pay the staff first. That's why I'm not getting paid." I responded, "Then I must get a job because we have maintenance charges on our co-op, and we have to eat." I was at home taking care of Gordon and wanted to help.

In 1961 Gordon was almost four years old. We agreed I would care for him during his formative years, recognizing that as a Black male, he required specific skills to confront challenges he would no doubt face later in life. Some might consider him a "mixed race" youngster, but in reality, he would always be perceived as Black by society. My first challenge was to pass the teacher's examination. Reviewing my college transcript, the only subject area where I qualified was social studies. Although a political science major, social sciences captured my interest. I took and passed the social studies exam.

I met with principal Charles Silverberg of the school across the street and said, "Mr. Silverberg, you have an integrated student body, but few, if any, Negro teachers. Your students need a role model, and, therefore, I think that you should hire me as a teacher.

He replied, "You have a license, but lack education courses, since you never taught."

I said, "Fine, I'll take education courses during the summer and come to work in the fall."

With twelve education credits at Hunter College, I began as a social studies teacher at Junior High School 126 in September of 1962.

I loved teaching. Although I never planned to teach, I found the challenge exhilarating. I loved working with the older students, helping them develop the critical thinking skills so necessary for success in life. A lifelong learner, I was both lucky and blessed to fall into such a rewarding occupation. A problem-solver by nature, I was constantly searching for new, creative situations.

In September 1965, as a teacher at John Bowne High School, I began taking courses at Columbia University under an African area studies program sponsored by the United States Government's Department of Cultural Affairs. After five years or so teaching at John Bowne, I took a leave of absence to become a full-time student of African Studies at Columbia, thereby supplementing my prior courses—also funded by the US government.

Meeting young Africans on trips abroad, my long-held interest in Africa was growing. I extended my leave of absence and in 1972 became director of the School Services Division of the African American Institute. In 1976, I left the institute to write my dissertation, honoring the five-year time limit Columbia University enforced for leaves of absence prior to dissertation completion.

In 1977, I returned to teaching and secured employment at the Far Rockaway High School because the chairman of the Social Studies Department at John Bowne High School had been appointed principal at Far Rockaway. Although New York City was in the midst of a fiscal crisis, he hired me as a social studies teacher. In 1978, I became executive assistant to the superintendent of high schools in Queens.

In 1980, I was appointed principal of Andrew Jackson High School. The point is that I knew the superintendent quite well because I had worked as his executive assistant for two years. His name was Aaron Maloff; we called him Archie.

During the 1979–1980 academic year, the Board of Education issued an edict requiring that all students be immunized against diphtheria, pertussis, and tetanus (DPT).

I was in and out of Andrew Jackson High School that summer, primarily preparing for the fall term, and students were not in school during the summer. When classes resumed in September of 1980, approximately 3,000 students were enrolled, but only half had their required immunization shots.

Archie Maloff called me into his office. "You're in violation of the rules of the New York City Board of

Education. You have about fifteen hundred students who are not immunized and, technically, they cannot be in the school building," he said. He presented me with a letter, which he delivered at this meeting, which read,

> Dear Dr. Rich,
> You're in violation of the rules and regulations of the New York City Board of Education, and you must comply immediately.
>
> Sincerely,
> Aaron Maloff

I was required to sign the letter, noting that I understood it would be placed in my file—my first disciplinary rebuke.

I asked myself, "What am I going to do?" Andrew Jackson was an "abandoned" school administered under the New York City Board of Education "Choice of Admissions" (COA) program. Although the school was in a primarily middle class African American neighborhood, Cambria Heights children could not attend.

In other words, striving middle class African American parents were prevented from sending their children to Andrew Jackson High. Rather, the majority were bused in from "The Projects"—a working-class, low-income neighborhood in South Jamaica, Queens. I spoke out against COA at a conference of the NAACP Legal Defense Fund, which resulted in another letter being placed in my file.

Principal for less than a month, I was suddenly confronted with 1,500 lower-income students requiring immunization. *This* was a challenge. I decided to immunize the 1,500 students. I phoned Dr. Saul Moroff, a good friend and member of ADA, the liberal political group with outstanding intellectuals and activists in its leadership, including Eleanor Roosevelt, Arthur Schlesinger Jr., John Kenneth Galbraith, and others. Marvin and I were very active in this organization.

Marvin, my dear husband, drummed into me that no one wants to hear about your *problems;* they want to hear about your *challenges* and *opportunities*. And so, from early on in our marriage, I never approached people for help with a "problem." Rather, I would say, "I have a challenge and need your help."

Describing my challenge, Saul assured me, "Evie, that is not a problem. I'm the supervisor of interns at Mount Sinai Hospital. Mount Sinai will donate the medicine you need, and I will bring interns to give the shots. All you have to do is organize the setting." I agreed, and we established a date.

Speaking to students weekly on our loudspeaker system, I would say, "Good morning. This is Dr. Rich, and I have several announcements." Now I added, "Dr. Moroff and his interns from Mount Sinai Hospital are coming to our school to give you your shots so that you can participate in our wonderful teaching and learning program." I did this every day for the next two weeks. I also told students, "Your homeroom teacher has permission slips for your shots. I want you to ask your mother, father, or guardian to sign them. As a reward, Burger King at the corner of 211th Street and Linden Boulevard is offering a free hamburger. Just show the voucher we provide you." Reaching and convincing the Burger King franchise owner to make this gesture is an example of local activism at work. You have to be creative.

Our auditorium accommodated eight hundred students. Directing my assistant principal to schedule students, I announced daily that Dr. Moroff had shown me the needle and that it was only two inches long. I also shared my fear of shots and big needles, reassuring students that this was a small needle; it wouldn't hurt, and they would receive a hamburger as a reward.

The big day came, and Dr. Moroff arrived with his interns. They immunized about 1,500 students for free. For a variety of reasons, a number of students lacked permission slips. Anticipating this challenge, surrogate parent members of the Parents' Association were present to sign permission slips for students who couldn't provide them.

My motto has always been: Overcome obstacles. By immunizing these students, we kept them in school. We also staggered redemption notices so that the restaurant was not overwhelmed. I felt pretty good about myself, my staff, and the school at the end of the day. I thanked Dr. Moroff, his interns, and Mount Sinai Hospital for their generosity.

We also closed school lunch periods. Many high schools in Queens had "open" lunch periods. They were neighborhood schools; students could return home for lunch. But our students, for the most part, did not live near the school. Rather, they typically raced to Jack in the Box, Arby's, or Burger King. At the urging of neighborhood groups, I declared that every student would henceforth eat lunch in school.

Doing so created a new set of challenges. The majority were eligible for free lunch and breakfast under Title I of the federal Elementary and Secondary School Act. However, my colleagues in Queens disliked the stigma of a free lunch program. I therefore asked them to give me all the breakfast-lunch vouchers they were *not* using. Their vouchers were constantly sufficient in number that everyone, not simply Title I eligible students, could enjoy two free meals daily.

The kids were initially quite upset when I told them they could not go out to lunch. So I appointed a committee of four teachers and four students, the latter tasked with telling our wonderful dietitian, Mrs. Clark, what the student body wanted to eat. (She chaired the committee.) These four canvassed others. For breakfast the majority wanted bacon, eggs, pancakes, and sausages. Mrs. Clark prepared it. Students were thrilled. For lunch, they wanted hamburgers and frankfurters. Again, they were ecstatic. With those free vouchers in hand, soon there was no stigma to eating at school. Our youth were previously eating potato chips and soda for lunch; no wonder they were having trouble learning. But kids like good food. And that's how I got away with insisting that all remain in school for lunch.

There are no *problems*—only *challenges and opportunities.*

12

Thwarting Drug Dealers at Andrew Jackson

Nineteen eighty represented the height of the crack epidemic in New York City and probably the nation. I had just been appointed principal of Andrew Jackson High School with a myriad of challenges on my plate. Confronting and preventing drug dealers from entering the school to sell marijuana and crack to my students was a priority. I needed a multifaceted defense/attack on these drug dealers. My objective was to permanently end their presence in Andrew Jackson High.

I considered every one of those students mine. I went from being a mother to one son to a mother of 3000-plus sons and daughters overnight. I never admitted that because surely students would try to take advantage if they knew that I considered them my students *and* my children.

The defense/attack was part of many strategies I developed. For example, I established what I called the "Principal's Fund." I asked financially solvent friends to help me take control of the school by contributing money to this fund. In retrospect, I don't recall how many contributed—perhaps twenty or thirty—or how much I was able to garner. I would say several thousand dollars.

The "Principal's Fund" helped me in many ways. For example, I purchased equipment to take ID photos of students on the first day of their September term. All who belonged inside the school building had an ID card with their name and picture. Student IDs also included their grade and official (homeroom) class. IDs were also created for the entire staff, including the principal. Everyone was required to display one to enter the school. This was the first part of my "defense."

Another was to identify and meet with the real student leaders of the school before the school year began. I asked student government members and others to identify those with reputations both good and bad—sports heroes, the toughest guys/girls, spokespersons for troubled students, and those shunted aside.

I developed a good relationship with the real school leaders. Before school opened, I brought them together with student government leaders to discuss mutual interests. I made it very clear that we were a team. I had confidence in them; it was really their school. But they must understand that I was the leader. Collectively, we designed what I called a "List of Expectations." *Expectations* was a euphemism for rules and regulations. One such expectation was: "I will wear my ID card in the building at all times."

Another "attack" strategy was building a parents' association. I asked the real leaders, "Which parents have shown interest in the school?" Reaching out, I told these parents, "The school cannot succeed without a vibrant parents' association. We must take control of the school, and I need your help."

A priority on my list was to clean the school both within and without. Outer walls were covered with graffiti. I directed the custodian and his staff to wash it all off, and the school began to shine. (Ultimately, the head custodian left because he was not sympathetic with my goals and expectations.) Again, I met with the real leaders, declaring, "We can't have the building covered with graffiti. I'm giving students a wall in the schoolyard." We had a big schoolyard because the school took up a whole city block. I explained, "This is your wall, and students can write anything they want to on it so long as it isn't obscene. However, you may *not* write on the rest of the school's walls. They are Dr. Rich's walls, my walls." When the school opened, it nearly glittered.

Another key expectation was that males could no longer wear hats in our school. I explained that it was my job to shape productive citizens, that men who wore hats to work were often in low-paying jobs. I was preparing them for remunerative jobs to support themselves and their families. Male students could not wear hats in the building.

I also tried to make friends with the police. The school was in the 105th precinct of the New York City Police Department. Making an appointment with the precinct commander, I asked him to assign a policeman to the school. Months later I learned that a policeman had been assigned to our school all along. I just never saw him because he spent his days in the furnace room. The school was heated with coal, believe it or not. We had a big furnace, with a man assigned to keep the fire burning and the building warm in winter. Discovering that the policeman was *hiding* in the furnace room all day, I made it in his best interests to leave the job.

When I introduced myself to the commander of the 105th Precinct, I said, "I would like you to assign two policemen to my school." This didn't happen for over a year, but at least he knew who I was.

* * *

On the opening day of school, students discovered a gleaming, beautifully maintained school building. It was very clear that they could not write on the walls. Students were also instructed to ask their parents to review and sign the "List of Expectations." For the most part they did so. With the Expectations List, ID card, clean edifice, and Parents' Association, I was able to set a new tone from the first day of school.

The school was designed with banks of doors for students to enter and exit. Three thousand students walked into one set of doors in the morning and left from another in the afternoon. The Expectations List stated that they would enter with a book in hand, as well as a notebook to write in, and they would *not* wear hats when they entered. Of course, some of the boys wore hats initially, but quickly got the message that hats were unacceptable. Over the course of the school year, I made it very clear that they were coming to work and expected to bring their "tools" with them—namely books and notebooks.

Drug dealers, for the most part, were not school students. They ventured in from outside. But with my new rules in place, they lacked ID cards. Secondly, they typically wore hats. Therefore, I was able to identify the drug dealers because they embraced hats and didn't have ID cards. When I found drug dealers in the school, I introduced myself, showed them my ID card and said, "I'd like to see your ID card, please." Of course, they didn't have one. I then said, "I am giving you a chance to leave. You have two choices: you can either leave the building now, or you can be arrested." Despite my petite stature, it was obvious that I was not afraid of them. Most left the building.

They were shocked to see me, because I made it my business to walk up and down the halls and stairwells. I did not spend the day sitting in my office. Students soon understood that they could find me in a hall during class changes. Although this was a very big building, I was all over it. (It was my exercise.)

On one of my daily trips around the school, I discovered a student writing on the wall. I could not believe it. "YOU are writing on MY wall!" I exclaimed. "I gave you a wall to write on." By this time, we had quite a crowd of students around us. "He wrote on my wall—on Dr. Rich's wall," I informed them. "We surely have to fix this."

I directed custodial staff to bring a bucket filled with cleaning items—Mr. Clean, Ajax, Lestoil, rags, the works—and the perpetrator cleaned the wall. Students who were watching went to their next class. The guilty student attended his with instructions to report the next day after the wall dried. The following day I pointed out to him that the rest of the wall—beyond the area that had been washed—was a different color. I gave him paint, and he painted the wall. It looked very nice when he finished. No other student ever wrote on my wall.

I had my first real victory when I confronted a young man without an ID card and wearing a hat. When I offered him the choice of leaving or being arrested, he challenged me. I escorted him to my office, called the police, and they arrested him. I led the way as police took him out in handcuffs. When students saw the police escort this young man out of the building, they were shaken. Word spread that this lady principal means business.

During the next few months, I took two other steps which helped cement my program against the drug dealers. They were selling marijuana, cigarettes, and crack. The first thing I did was to take the handles off the outside doors of the school, except for the front door where I stationed security guards. No one could enter the building from the various exits/entrances except by way of the front door. That was a big shock to students; doors could be opened from the inside but not from the outside.

It was an important strategy. Drug dealers could no longer slip into the building at the beginning of the day because they didn't have ID cards. They would wait until classes started, then try to enter. A few students tried to assist by opening doors from the inside. But I directed our security staff of eight guards to monitor exits in a way that students never knew when a security guard would catch them opening the doors. Those caught opening the doors from the inside were suspended. I issued numerous suspensions my first year.

To further thwart drug dealers, I invited undercover policemen into the building to pose as students. I met with the commander of the 111th Precinct, where New York City stationed its Drug Prevention Program serving Queens. I explained that I wanted four young policemen to pose as students in order to identify those selling drugs to the other students. We gave them ID cards and a class schedule; they attended classes with the other students. No one knew they were actually police officers. They identified drug dealers among my students.

I approached this challenge externally and internally: externally by taking the handles off the outside doors, and internally by stationing undercover policemen. Over the course of the year, I rid the building of these drug dealers.

Another challenge I faced was the presence of guns. As a result of the city's student placement program, youth came from all over Queens. A few brought guns to school. However, I quickly identified those students. Almost always a "he," rather than a "she," they brought guns to show other students. They didn't keep the gun in their school bag. The whole idea was to show it off to others.

Since I walked the building all day, students confided in the hallway that there was a gun in the school. Other students shared the exact location or one of my undercover policemen sent word. I quickly went after the culprit. Walking into the classroom, announcing myself to the teacher, and greeting the students, I said, "I would like to talk with Mr. X in my office." Taking the student into my office, along with a security guard, I asked him to show me the gun. Admitting he had a gun, the student showed it to me. Once he did, I had the police arrest him. Police took the student out in handcuffs, and I walked in front of them.

I dealt with drug dealers and students with guns by identifying them and forcing them out of the building in handcuffs. Word went out across the borough, "Don't mess with this lady because she means business." I'm proud to say that no student in my school was ever shot or attacked with a gun or knife. Plus, I successfully confronted the drug dealers.

Teachers were not always on my side. Upset with my rule banning hats in the school building, a small group reported me to the American Civil Liberties Union (ACLU). I'm a member of the ACLU. The head of the ACLU in New York sent word that she wanted to meet with me. She attended my college but didn't know me. Arriving at Andrew Jackson, she asserted, "Dr. Rich, I understand that you are depriving students in your school of their First Amendment rights by telling them they cannot wear hats in the school."

I replied, "I believe in the First Amendment just like you do. At a recent faculty meeting I asked teachers how many of their children wear hats to school. None wore hats in the building. Where in the Constitution does it say that you can wear hats at Andrew Jackson High School? Come back when the founding fathers rewrite the Constitution to say that students in the Andrew Jackson High School can wear hats. But until then, I'm the principal, I'm the educational leader, and in my school, male students do not wear hats."

I felt and continue to believe that an effective educational environment requires three core principles: respect, recognition, and rewards. My reputation for getting rid of drug dealers and guns must have spread. A few years later, New York City Real Estate Board members asked to meet. They arrived in a huge, black limousine. They wanted to know how I succeeded in driving out drug dealers from Andrew Jackson High School and how I was able to make our school a safer environment. The New York City drug crisis made it difficult to operate their multimillion-dollar buildings. I was happy to share my strategies. They were pleased with my suggestions and invited me to join the National Association Against Drug Abuse Problems (NADAP), which they supported to fight drug dealers. Ultimately, I became co-chair of the group. Meanwhile, the drug dealers stayed away from my school.

Jackson was built in the 1930s. It was a beautifully constructed school with bannisters made of brass. Students cleaned the dirty bannisters until they gleamed. They were also accustomed to throwing papers on the floor, but I convinced them to stop. Visitors were shocked. Everything had a place. Dirty Depression-era murals decorated the cafeteria. Using the Principal's Fund, I paid an expert to clean the murals. Entering the school lifted your spirits. Semi-detached houses surrounded the school, but people were afraid to live in them. The head of the Brooklyn Union Gas Company asked to meet. "Based on your success with the school, we want to create the Andrew Jackson Cinderella Project by facilitating low-cost mortgages for these homes," he explained. Suddenly, the neighborhood was transformed. Kids were proud of their school. Previously, nobody tried to help them, but now they had a principal who cared.

In 2024, former students organized a fifty-year celebration honoring the school, themselves, and me—with several hundred attending, a float on wheels, the marching band, a football game, and wonderful food. I was accorded seats of honor on the float and football game. Several alumni told me, "We thought you were so mean, but after you left we realized how important you were to the school."

13

Dr. Rich and the Police

In New York City, today and yesterday, people of color have had very negative interactions with the police. However, my story with the police is just the opposite. Rather than hiding in our furnace room, officers were soon volunteering to teach and mentor students.

As indicated above, Andrew Jackson High School sits in a part of Queens the police consider dangerous. Once a thriving White middle-class enclave, Cambria Heights is a Black middle-class community with a significant crime problem. During my time as principal, students typically came from low-income families. Most were from single parent households. They seldom achieved in school, and many were prone to negative behaviors.

Shortly after the 1980 opening, I met with the 105th Precinct Commander to request the assignment of two policemen. Unresponsive, he insisted that an officer *was* assigned to the school. As I soon learned, he arrived surreptitiously each day and spent his on-duty hours in the furnace room. Therefore, many months into the term, I requested a second meeting with the commander and with the patrolmen at roll call. Police meet for the news of the day prior to roll call. During my remarks, I invited them to work with me.

They knew I meant business because I summoned police to arrest drug dealers trespassing on school property. Through my talk, I convinced officers to volunteer at the school, promising that, in return for their service, I would help them pass the sergeant's exam. To my delight, six volunteers signed up to work the three shifts: 8:00 a.m. to 4:00 p.m., 4:00 p.m. to 12:00 a.m., and 12:00 a.m. to 8:00 a.m.

I asked several of the more effective instructors to teach these officers how to teach. I also asked these officers to spend several hours observing teachers whose performance I felt was exemplary. We held post-observation conferences where I pointed out the outstanding features of the lessons they observed.

We initiated a new course in the school called "Law & Society." I designed the curriculum with several teachers and the policemen. One volunteer officer worked with a teacher from 8:00 a.m. to 4:00 p.m., developing the curriculum for our ninth grade students. Each class of about thirty students spent a week together learning about "Law & Society" instead of attending their usual courses. The curriculum consisted of varied topics, including:

1. The role of the police in the larger society—enforce the laws; protect people and property; ensure safety.
2. The role of the police in the school—support assigned security guards; make arrests of trespassers where necessary; respond to emergencies.
3. How to interact with policemen/women outside of the school building—listen to directives; speak calmly; understand restrictions of police power.
4. Policemen/women as citizens—viewing them as fathers/mothers; members of the community.

Over the course of the year, volunteer officers taught all ninth grade students in the school, as youth cycled through the course. Law and Society epitomized the role of police at our school. While one officer taught with the teacher, the other carried out his assigned duties, enabling students to see for themselves what the police did in the school.

Two officers worked the 4:00 p.m. to 12:00 p.m. shift. They supervised extracurricular activities, including basketball games in the school gym, football games on the athletic field adjacent to the school, and homecoming events. They also interacted with parents who were police personnel. At the beginning of each school semester, students completed a questionnaire. One of the questions was: What does your parent or guardian do for a living? Identifying parents who were policemen or women, I hosted events where police assigned to the school met the police parents of children in the school.

Police assigned to the 12:00 a.m. to 8:00 a.m. shift worked primarily in the larger community around the school. And, as I told my students, they should not be out past midnight. The Law & Society course taught the youngsters what to do if they were driving their family's car on the Grand Central Parkway and were stopped by the police. Information gleaned through this one-week course resulted in Speech 101. The New York State Board of Regents mandated students to take an English course every semester. Passing grades for four years of English were required for graduation. Unilaterally, I turned one of those English courses into a speech course and hired two speech teachers. Students were introduced to the idea of speaking the English language correctly. To achieve a passing grade in the course, they were required to give a two- to three-minute speech in class, in front of the teacher, their peers, and me. We jointly decided whether they passed the course. Each class consisted of about thirty students or so. We spent the last three or four weeks of the term with students giving their speeches.

I explained to the students that one of the reasons I wanted them to make this speech was to present themselves effectively. I provided examples illustrating how this would help them, including: applying for a job; if they were stopped by the police, arrested, or had to appear at a court hearing; or if they had to present themselves in some other formal venue.

Youngsters learned about the police, about the court, about the role of the police in society in our Law & Society course, but they were really equipped to better present themselves effectively in legal situations or in the workplace as a result of the speech classes. The policemen and women assigned to the school developed very positive relationships with the students because they saw these students every day. A number of officers had such good relationships with the students that they became mentors for the youngsters. They would see the kids in the school building, in the community, or they would see them at a ball game, and they began to develop an affinity for students that was very positive.

One such policeman was Charles Wells (now deceased). Officer Wells was a Youth Outreach Officer at Jackson High School. He taught the Law &Society

class for ten years and mentored students. Many began to feel differently about the police. As a result, school disciplinary incidents plummeted. Criminal activities in the neighborhood also decreased significantly. I suspect that a number of youngsters considered doing something that they ought not be doing. Encountering a police officer they recognized often turned the tide.

What were the results of this police presence in the school? Undoubtedly, the relationship between students and the police, both in the school building and in the larger community, improved dramatically, creating a positive perception of police rather than a negative one. The program also added to my many duties and responsibilities, since I also taught after-school courses helping our officers prepare for the sergeant's exam. I never had a problem with recruiting new police because every officer I tutored passed the sergeant's exam—the very first time. Being a police officer at Andrew Jackson High School was transformed into a positive assignment rather than one to be avoided.

I like to believe that the relationships I built with the police had a long-term positive effect on the students, as well as the image the school projected in the community and the larger borough. In this era, there are legitimate concerns about police playing negative roles. I believe that such actions derive from poor internal police leadership and supervision, reinforced by negativity within the police union. The union should understand its important role in developing humane, sympathetic, and empathetic police officers. If it did, things would be very different and public support would grow.

Finally, my efforts to build a more effective school occurred against a background of institutional racism—both on the part of my superiors within the Department of Education, certain teachers within the school, and leaders of the teachers' union. There was resistance to my initiatives up and down the line. I was targeted by the union, the United Federation of Teachers, and by the Board of Education as well. I was always breaking rules and receiving letters in my file for actions I felt best served our students and the school.

I tried to entice the teachers to join me in my many creative efforts. Some did. But there was union leadership within the school and union members who did not believe in the students or in our joint mission to educate these teenagers as productive citizens.

I am very pro-union personally and interact with union members throughout the city and nation. I am a proud union member. I have thus put my experience with the UFT behind me and moved on. In retrospect, had the UFT cooperated rather than resisted our initiatives, I believe Jackson would have flourished as an even more effective school.

My tenure at Jackson did not end on a happy note. When I learned that a teacher was sexually abusing a student, I insisted that he be transferred. My supervisor was not supportive. The union said that if the teacher was transferred, I, too, could no longer serve in the school. The union was very powerful. I could not publicly charge the teacher because—despite how despicable this action was—I feared for his safety.

In retrospect, I believe that racism had a lot to do with my departure. I worked tirelessly with students, staff, parents and community to change the school's image. Indeed, it had changed. The school's reputation grew—in a good way. But I paid a big price.

I was fortunate to find a new job as dean of the Hunter College Campus Schools, two laboratory schools for gifted K-12 students. I moved on to new adventures in a new venue. However, the most rewarding and challenging job I ever had was serving students at Andrew Jackson High School. They were all my kids, and I loved them.

14

Confronting Giftedness

Lin-Manuel Miranda, the famed creator of the musical *Hamilton*, was only in second grade. Yet my fortuitous position at Hunter College helped nurture his talents. Shape one life; you shape the world. In Lin-Manuel Miranda's case, his talent reverberated throughout the globe. He wasn't the only one.

In 1985, I spoke on an education panel with Donna Shalala, then president of the college. She phoned the next day with an offer: to lead the two K-12 laboratory schools on campus. Serving intellectually gifted children, global scholars used them for baseline research. But the schools had few African American or Hispanic children. Shalala was not interested in minority students per se, but only in gifted minority children who could pass Hunter's rigorous entrance exams.

At the time, I doubted the concept of "giftedness." It is challenging for any child, much less a Black or Hispanic youngster and a four-year-old at that, to be deemed "gifted." Nevertheless, the handwriting was on the wall. My mother was upset because I lost a great deal of weight during my time at Jackson. I wasn't plump to begin with. I was also fighting the teachers' union (UTF) for insisting on the transfer of a teacher for unacceptable behavior. Board of Education staff secretly approached the Parents' Association president and at least one city council person to secure support against me.

Seeing a new opportunity and simultaneously an escape from this tension, I accepted the challenge. Then-Provost Tilden LeMelle and President Donna Shalala were extremely supportive. I assumed the post in July 1985 and retired in April 1992. The Hunter College Campus Schools (HCCS) consist of an elementary school and a high school. The elementary school serves Manhattan students from Pre-K (nursery) through grade six. The high school caters to students from grade seven to twelve who live in NYC's five boroughs. My responsibilities included supervising the two principals, admissions director, physical plant supervisor, and outreach director, as well as external relations.

Admittedly, it was rocky. My duties were revised on several occasions, each time diminishing my role—so much so that in 1992, when there was an offer of early retirement for faculty and staff, I left. I made enemies primarily due to my refusal to bend admission requirements. So-called powerful individuals demanded guideline waivers. I refused.

The laboratories were and remain prestigious public schools. They surely rank among the best public schools in New York City, including Bronx Science, Stuyvesant, and Brooklyn Technical High Schools. However, tuition is free, whereas tuition in outstanding private schools in New York City is astronomical. Parents with children in the Campus Schools save hundreds of thousands of dollars. In some sense these schools fly under the radar. Poor and working-class parents seldom hear about this option. But the politically powerful are well aware. To have a child accepted and educated at Hunter was and is a coup.

The student body for the 1985–86 academic year had already been selected. Admission to the elementary school occurred at two levels: first in the nursery (Pre-K) area and secondly in kindergarten. The school had about six hundred students. Thirty-two attended the nursery school; the remaining were in grades K to 6. Five hundred and forty attended the high school, grades 7 to 12.

The preschool admissions process was complex. It is very difficult—if not impossible—to determine whether a four-year-old is gifted. Pre-K and kindergarten admission criteria were based on an IQ test (99 percent on the Stanford-Binet) and a group interview. A faculty committee reviewed Stanford-Binet results, examined performance exams, and made final choices. High school admission was based on a fifth grade reading exam and scores on HCHS faculty exam.

Elementary age children and faculty were less ethnically diverse than the high school, with roughly a 5 percent minority for both in 1985. When I left, it was about 30 percent. The high school ethnic breakdown was about 25 percent in 1985 because there were many Asian students. When I departed, it was about 35 percent, with an increasing number of Asian youth.

Establishing an outreach program to recruit gifted minority children into the elementary school, I asked three minority faculty to define "gifted." We developed a one-page statement of gifted behaviors. I then asked three New York City radio stations catering to minority audiences—KISS-FM, WWRL, and WLIB—to have me as a guest on their shows. Speaking about giftedness, I invited listeners to a Hunter evening with psychologists and faculty members to explore whether their child was gifted.

Two hundred parents showed up. We had a wonderful evening—and repeated it annually for the next six years. Psychologists present identified specific behaviors indicating giftedness among minorities. Over the years, we significantly increased the number of African American and Hispanic children, as well as other minorities, in the elementary school selection pool.

A Black Parents' Association serving both schools was established before I arrived. An outstanding group of parents distinguished in a variety of fields, all were deeply committed to the success of their children. We met periodically, informally, and they provided support. The single most-important factor in shaping the attitude and educational performance of children is the behavior of parents. Together, we designed a program to help minority parents nurture the gifted behaviors of their toddlers. For example, we prepared a list of children's books featuring minority boys and girls. We developed a list of museum exhibitions to excite their children and urged parents to obtain a public library card, as well as one for their child.

I encountered hostility from several parents at the increasing numbers of minority children on campus. In their limited view, minorities could not possibly be gifted. Remember, this was the early 1980s. On the positive side, look at the sea change in our society today.

Sometimes children left the school—their parents moved away, or the students were unhappy for a variety of reasons. I therefore created a waiting list for children we identified as gifted but had no space for after the initial performance test. One such child was second grader Lin-Manuel Miranda. A few parents were unhappy. They approached me privately, questioning both timing and the issue of giftedness. I said, "Listen, he's very gifted. He was on the wait list, and we have room now because a student has left the school. We've admitted him." And, indeed, he turned out to be highly gifted. Lin-Manuel Miranda spent ten years at Hunter Campus schools—graduating from its high school. He went on to become an accomplished playwright, songwriter, rapper, actor, and filmmaker who won a Pulitzer Prize, five Grammy awards, three Tony awards, and more. Shining a light on students at a young age can make a huge difference in their lives.

Another graduate who had an equally distinguished career: US Supreme Court Justice Elena Kagan. Her mother, Gloria Kagan, taught sixth grade at the Campus Schools for many years. Her father, Robert Kagan, served on a committee I created to find a new location for the schools or build a new school.

I also brought in a blind elementary age child and a blind high school student. Again, a few parents were upset. They asked me how a blind youngster could be gifted? I said, "Well, why not? He has a disability, and he can't see, but that doesn't mean he's not gifted."

By contrast, the majority of parents were supportive. While I never explicitly discussed my minority goals, it was obvious, and they backed my efforts. I reported to the Dean of Programs in Education, an African American who also believed in exceptions. For the most part, African American elementary school students, in particular, did not score above the cutoff required for high school admission. In my view, these youngsters were gifted and could succeed. The dean concurred that our exam content could be part of the problem. Frankly, promoting them was also an effective strategy for diversifying the high school. As far as I know, they all graduated.

A significant number of Hispanic and African American youngsters scored above the 99th percentile on the New York City reading examination in grade five, but did not pass the examination for admission to Hunter in the sixth grade. A provision providing admission for a limited number of economically disadvantaged students yielded very few African American and Hispanic students. Rather, they were overwhelmingly White and understandably so, because there are more White poor and working-class families in New York City.

As noted, the high school admissions exam created by faculty was very difficult. When I asked the head of the College Board administering the SAT to review the exam, he shared it with his colleagues. They agreed the exam was too hard for sixth graders. Several adults on his team failed the test. To win admission, one had to score above the cutoff on the multiple-choice exam and write a passing essay.

At my urging, questions reflecting Hispanic, African American, and other cultures were added, for example, poetry written by minority Americans and essay questions reflecting their history. Minority youngsters performed much better on these questions. While I regret my inability to significantly expand the percentage of minorities passing the entrance exam, the numbers generally reflected the New York population at the time. When I left, the percentage of Black students was about 8 percent, Asian students at 26 percent, Hispanic students about 5 percent, and the rest were White students. I culled these percentages from an annual survey (BEDS) conducted by the New York State Education Department.

A group of parents whose youngsters did not pass the high school admissions test demanded their children's test papers under the Freedom of Information Law (FOIL). Courts rebuffed these efforts. When we explained the design and execution of the test, the relevant courts upheld our decision to refuse dissemination.

When two elementary and high school principals were denied reappointment in 1987—public explanations were not required—the Parents' Association went on the offensive. Charges were leveled at me for replacing White principals with Black principals, and at the dean who took the decision. But that's not what we did. In fact, the two principals we hired were White.

I also realized that the math team and calculus classes lacked young women. When questioned, the mathematics department chair told me that the girls were not as smart as the boys when it came to math, even though she was a female and a HCHS alumna. I teamed up with a faculty member on a grant for two calculus classes: one restricted to girls, and the other with boys and girls. We conducted this experiment for several years. The result: the girls in the all-female calculus classes performed much better than the girls in the classes with the boys. Girls also joined the math team.

I prefer to look at these years as a glass three-fourths full. We made tremendous strides in opening the minds of parents and encouraging talented youth of all persuasions. Skeptical about giftedness at the outset, I became a fierce advocate for thousands who would have otherwise missed the opportunity to develop their gifts in such a creative setting. The Hunter College Campus Schools serve a vital role, and I support them to this day.

15

We Weren't Helicopter Parents

Parents in this era tend to hover over their offspring. They become deeply involved in their children's schooling, friendships, sports, as well as other activities. Marvie and I were definitely not helicopter parents. I wasn't interested in marriage nor in raising a family when I met Marvie, but he convinced me otherwise. Marvie and I were married in Philadelphia in 1956—a year when interracial marriage was still illegal in twenty-four states.

Both Marvie and I had a passion for helping others—making our country a better place for *all* people. When I discovered a year into our marriage that I was pregnant, I felt betrayed by the medical science of contraception. Marvie, who grew up in a large, loving family, was ecstatic at the prospect of becoming a father. "Don't worry," he said. "I know exactly what to do." Indeed, he did know exactly what to do.

Our son, Gordon Alexander Rich, was born in November 1957. We lived in New York City—a liberal city in a liberal state; however, there were still very few multiracial children at that time. I wanted to raise an intellectually curious, achievement-oriented son who could handle being Black in a White world. Marvie hoped to nurture a compassionate son who cared deeply about others.

In April of 1958, we were the first tenants to move into our co-op, Queensview West, a lower-middle-income cooperative community in Queens, New York. Soon there were at least twelve boys and girls our son's age in our complex. We had a two-bedroom apartment and a nice playground with equipment geared toward young children. There I met my closest friend, Irma Horowitz, who lived in the building next door. Irma had a daughter, Amy, who was five months younger than Gordon. They, too, became fast friends.

Irma maintained a kosher home and taught me a great deal about being kosher. Marvie was raised in a kosher home, but that part of Judaism was not important to him. He explained that he was a cultural Jew rather than a religious one. Irma and her husband, Jack, joined us for meals which were obviously not kosher—like baked ham and potato salad.

Despite having very little money, we were imaginative parents raising an only child who was Black. We went to the public library and signed out books I read to Gordon. Marvie rushed home from work to play with Gordie, change diapers, bathe him, and plan expeditions. These included trips to Rainey Park (near the East River), to the lumberyard, and to the supermarket. Before their grocery trips, I constructed maps identifying the location of each food group. (I still have such a map.)

There were no other Black or mixed-race children in our co-op at the time. When Gordon was about ten years old, another mixed-race couple moved in. Their son, David Hodges, became one of Gordon's lifelong friends. Almost every day at 4:00 p.m. we had tea. That's largely because we had tea every day at 4:00 p.m. at Bryn Mawr College. I invited one or two of Gordon's young friends. We had tea and cinnamon toast. We often put fresh lemon juice in the tea. One day I substituted fresh orange slices. Both mothers of the two children called to chastise me for setting a bad example. Their sons complained about tea with cinnamon toast, much less orange slices.

When Gordon was about two years old, I began reading the *New York Times* to him. I read it to him daily until he was about five. Subsequently I read it to him regularly—but not at the same time each day. We then discussed the articles. Some stories interested him more than others. Of great interest was the Federal Reserve System. He was fascinated by the differences between monetary and fiscal policy. By age five, he had a savings account in a local bank.

One day he made a deposit and asked the teller to show him all of his money. I explained that the bank did not physically possess his money, but instead had funds equivalent to his deposit; his money had been loaned out to other customers to generate interest. The teller could show him money at hand. He was not satisfied. I reassured him that he could withdraw his full amount anytime. In retrospect, I now understand that this was an early indication of his burgeoning interest in finance.

* * *

In 1960, the sit-ins began in the South. Marvie was often on the road training CORE sit-in participants in nonviolent techniques. I tried to help in many ways while staying in the city. I took Gordon in his stroller to picket lines or other demonstrations, because we did not have the money to pay a babysitter. The cover photo for this book shows us picketing American Airlines for failing to hire Negro pilots. I'm pushing Gordon in his stroller, and he is holding a sign announcing, I WANT TO GROW UP TO BE AN AIRLINE PILOT.

Occasionally, Irma watched over Gordon when we left him at home. At two and a half, he attended the neighborhood preschool in the afternoon. We had trouble scrounging up tuition because Marvie believed that CORE should pay other staff members first. For Marvie, his civil rights work wasn't a job. It was a calling.

In July 1962, Marvie was arrested in Albany, Georgia. Although the Queensview West community rallied to our support, I feared that preschool children would tell Gordon his father was in jail. I decided to tell him myself. We had an extensive conversation one evening. The charges against Marvie were parading without a permit, leading a demonstration, and disorderly conduct. I explained that there were "good" laws and "bad" laws; his father broke some bad laws. I pointed out that Marvie's conduct was never disorderly.

I discussed the role of skin color in our society. I noted that Gordie's skin color was darker than Marvie's, while my skin color was darker than his. Marvie was White, and we were Black. I said that one's skin color often determines what you can do, where you can live and even who you could marry. Gordon listened intently but said very little. That Saturday when we were picketing on 125th Street in Harlem, Gordon pointed out all the "brown" people like him and me.

The time soon came for Gordon to go to school. Problems immediately appeared. PS 83—his assigned neighborhood school—was falling apart. I knew nothing about schools then, but was always on the lookout for a challenge. I talked to co-op parents with youngsters slated to attend PS 83. After a series of meetings in my apartment, we decided to build a new elementary school.

Of course, I had never built a school, but relished the challenge. I went to the library, visited the Board of Education, and talked with architects. Location presented a problem. Ravenswood, a middle-income public housing project, was across the street. During the thirty-eight years Marvie and I lived in Queensview West, Ravenswood had a wonderful reputation. Our public library was centrally based within Ravenswood. It was very well maintained, offering varied programs for its tenants. Ravenswood leaders were highly knowledgeable politically. Visitors from around the country and beyond came to view the project. Queensview West's children played with Ravenswood children, both on its grounds and ours.

However, located just several blocks south and beneath the Queensboro Bridge, stood Queensbridge, a low-income public housing project. I wanted to establish a school that would cater to children from both housing communities. This idea did not excite Queensview West or Ravenswood parents. Reinforced by a small group of supporters, I spent hours and days trying to convince them of the benefits. Ultimately, after a prolonged struggle, we succeeded. When PS 76 opened as a University Teacher Education Center (SUTEC) School in partnership with the Queens College Department of Education, Gordon was in the second grade. Attending school alongside Black, White, and other minority children, Gordon received an exceptional education from a team of outstanding teachers.

When Gordon was six years old, he expressed a keen interest in playing the piano. To support his burgeoning passion, I approached a neighbor whose daughters disliked their piano. I offered to buy it, and she agreed to sell it to me for $200 on an installment plan. A piano teacher in our co-op soon became Gordon's tutor. Gordon was enamored with the piano. He played tirelessly daily for several years. However, one day, his teacher informed me that Gordon missed his lesson, which was surprising given his love for playing. When I asked him about it, Gordon explained that he didn't attend because the teacher had already taught him all she knew.

I found a new teacher, Mr. Bernard Seiffert. He came from the Bronx to Astoria to work with Gordon. For his sixteenth birthday, Marvie, Gordon, and I visited the Steinway store on 57th Street in New York City. We couldn't afford a grand piano, so we bought Gordon a new upright Steinway piano. Mr. Seiffert visited the store previously, played all the uprights, and told us which piano Gordon should select. He was right.

Gordon loved playing Chopin's etudes. While his preference was for classical music, he frequently enjoyed playing Gershwin's jazz composition, "Rhapsody in Blue." He selected Swarthmore College, in part because the Lang Music building was equipped with Steinway grand pianos and open all night. In the evening, Gordon visited the building to play. Gordon greatly appreciated Mr. Seiffert's guidance as a teacher and continued lessons during school vacations. After graduation, Gordon engaged in four-hand piano pieces—two people playing simultaneously. Years later, after earning a good deal of money, he bought himself a Steinway grand piano.

Gordon developed an interest in fine dining and culinary arts at a young age, specializing in French cuisine. Although his father and I were not particularly interested in food, inviting wealthy friends to dinner proved a successful strategy for raising money for CORE. Gordon crafted remarkable dishes, often inspired by watching Julia Child on television or reading her book, *Mastering the Art of French Cooking*. Gordon bravely invited Paula

Peck, author of several cookbooks, to dinner. She complimented him after the meal.

One of the joys of living in Queensview was our relationship with Mel and Lillian Abrams. Many friends had a positive impact on Gordon as he matured, but none more than Mel and Lillian. We met them when we moved into Queensview West. They lived next door.

The Abrams quickly became Gordon's surrogate grandparents. Mel enjoyed playing cards—he taught Gordon how to play Casino and other card games. Recognizing Gordon's curiosity and sharp memory, he taught him bridge when Gordon was perhaps eight years old.

Soon Mel began taking Gordon to competitive bridge tournaments as his partner, placing a thick phone book on Gordon's chair so he would be at table height. Imagine the look on the other players' faces when this elderly Jewish man walked into a tournament with a young African American child as his partner. And they won. Gordon attained many master bridge points at a young age.

Marvie and I supported Gordon's many interests, but we certainly didn't hover over him. We wanted him to become an independent, resourceful person. For instance, Gordon was passionate about tennis. He began by hitting tennis balls against backboards in the neighborhood park. Then he moved on to playing on courts a bit farther away. When Gordon decided to play competitively in the twelve-and-under category in New York/New Jersey, he had to decipher public transportation to play.

We helped defray transportation costs, but he traveled on his own. When Gordon asked to attend a two-week summer tennis camp, we paid the camp fees and dropped him off. Fetching Gordon at the end of the summer, we watched him play in the finals. He was a fine tennis player. Gordon lost twice in local NY tournaments to John McEnroe, who would become the number one player in the world from 1980 to 1982.

We enrolled him in a rigorous junior high and high school program at Friends Seminary in Manhattan. Most of the schools we applied to were seeking students from working-class Black backgrounds. Marvin and I were both working at the time, so we could afford the tuition. Gordon navigated two subway trains from our apartment in Queens to Friends Seminary in Manhattan. I showed him how to do it once and then he was on his own. Intellectually challenged, he flourished at the Friends Seminary and formed lifelong friendships. In the decades since Gordon's death, two of his best school buddies visit whenever they're in New York. Gil Fleitas lives in California and David Hirst across the world in Hong Kong.

We are a family of readers. Marvie read everything. Gordon adopted Marvie's habit of rereading books he loved. For his birthday, we gave him a new set of Tolkien's *The Lord of the Rings* Trilogy. He set them aside and continued to reread his old paperback versions—books without covers or even the beginning pages. Gordon knew them by heart, so missing pages did not bother him.

Marvie, Gordon, and I watched news and "special" programs on television. We subscribed to liberal magazines like *Dissent* and *The New York Review of Books*. Gordon read these as well. We had interesting, sometimes heated, conversations at dinner about an issue. Gordon frequently disagreed with teachers, particularly his social studies teacher who was also head of the Middle School. Although only twelve or thirteen years old, Gordon was accustomed to being treated as an equal with his views respected. He easily defended his perspective and challenged others. As a social studies teacher, I taught my students to think critically and creatively. I loved an argument, and they knew it.

One day Gordon told me that he just couldn't take his social studies instructor anymore. The class was studying World War I and discussing military campaigns. The discussion centered on the weaponry used by the Germans. Challenging the teacher, Gordon provoked a heated conversation. He was right about the facts. "Evie," he insisted. "You must do something." He almost always called me Evie. (He only called me "Mother" when he was mad at me.)

I loved my son. I told him that I would create a voodoo doll and make this teacher very sick. Gordon watched while I created the doll from scraps I had in the house—a single black sock of Marvie's, a single black glove of mine, buttons from my sewing can, etc. I told him that I needed something she touched, since I had no access to her fingernails. He gave me a homework paper the teacher graded. I stuffed it inside the sock.

I am a "hat" person. I have many hats and a collection of hat pins for special hats. I selected a large, ivory hat pin and stuck it into the voodoo doll three times. The next day the teacher was absent from school. I stuck the doll again—this time four times. The next day Gordon was solemn. "She's in intensive care," he announced. "Please don't kill her!" I assured him, "Don't worry. I'll make her well."

I took a beaker from my medicine cabinet, filled it with warm salt water and dropped salt water on the doll, four drops in all. Gordon smiled. "Do you think it will work?" he asked. "Have confidence," I assured him. The next day Gordon came home from school, all excited. "She's out of intensive care," he reported. I repeated the procedure, this time using only three drops of warm salt water with the dropper. The following day he reported that she was discharged from the hospital.

Now, let me reassure you that I don't know a thing about voodoo. I just wanted to help my son. It worked, yes, but that was all accidental. Of course, Gordon thought that I had magical powers but, to be honest, he thought there wasn't anything I couldn't do, if I really wanted to.

There is an end to this account. Friends, like most schools, has Open School Day and Open School Night. When Gordon and I appeared, I noticed that none of the students or parents sat next to us. We were surrounded by empty seats. When we arrived home, I asked Gordon for an explanation. He said that he had no idea. I asked whether he told anyone about the voodoo doll. He admitted that he told all his friends about it because none of them really liked this teacher. I was upset with him because he had shared personal information with his classmates. I asserted that I would think twice before coming to his aid the next time.

I have looked for the doll, which his wife, MaryAnn, gave me when Gordon passed away. So far, I've been unable to find it.

During his time at Friends, Gordon interacted with many wealthy parents. Gordon observed that while they were significantly wealthier than his own, they did not appear to be more intelligent. One day he told his father that he did not intend to be the one asking for money for good causes. He wanted to be the person with money—giving to worthy causes.

Always following an accelerated learning curve, Gordon left Friends during his third year of high school. He applied to Harvard at sixteen, but the university suggested he spend another year in high school, after which they would automatically accept him. Instead, Gordon enrolled at Swarthmore, a small liberal arts college south of Philadelphia, which was willing to accept him without a high school diploma. Gordon majored in mathematics and economics, graduating Phi Beta Kappa with high honors in both subjects. He again flourished, made lifelong friends, and met his future wife, MaryAnn.

During his senior year, Gordon decided the best way to earn money was to become a lawyer or businessman. Law degrees (JDs) are typically obtained after three years of study. Master of Business degrees are earned after two years of study. At the time, Harvard had a special program for a select few where a JD/MBA degree could be obtained in just four years. Gordon applied, was accepted, and completed both his law and business degrees in four years.

After graduation from Harvard, Gordon accepted a job at Skadden, Arps, Meagher, Slate and Flom, practicing Merger and Acquisition Law—generating thick documents to blend companies. (I was then principal of Andrew Jackson High School; a number of lawyers at Gordon's office supported me pro bono. If I was in doubt on issues, they advised on how to proceed.) He was subsequently hired by Credit Suisse/First Boston to manage Mergers and Acquisitions.

He married MaryAnn, they had two sons, built a home, and led busy suburban lives. A middle school social studies teacher, MaryAnn directed much of their home life. Gordon was co-head of two departments at Credit Suisse. When he wasn't traveling for work, Gordon commuted daily from his suburban dream home. On a typical fall afternoon, Gordon played tennis with gusto in the morning, followed by a quick swim. Then it was off to the local grocery store with his young sons to purchase fresh ingredients for dinner. Gordon's enjoyment of cooking continued as an adult. During weekends, he created amazing dinners culled from *Gourmet* magazine recipes or from the many cookbooks he acquired. Afternoons were filled with their sons' town sports games.

One Saturday in November 2000 began as a typical Saturday. Family breakfast, tennis, swim, grocery shop. In the afternoon, Gordon intensely watched their twelve-year-old son's soccer game while asking suburban moms about the local gossip. MaryAnn attended their nine-year-old son's game.

Returning home, Gordon cooked dinner for his sons while MaryAnn explained bedtime routines to the teenage babysitter. They were meeting several of Gordon's coworkers for dinner. They had a wonderful meal, a fun evening, but both were exhausted. Gordon insisted on driving. He planned to awaken his wife when they reached New Jersey. Gordon put the car on cruise control. Partway home, he must have nodded off. The car veered off the road, careening into a ditch. MaryAnn survived with minor injuries. Gordon, who had recently celebrated his forty-third birthday, did not. In an instant, our vibrant son, our only child, was gone.

Gordon's zest for life, quest for knowledge, his intellect, his passion for sports lives on through his sons and grandsons. His older son, Maximilian, is a good cook, a talented lawyer, devoted husband, father, son, and grandson. Max followed in his father's footsteps, becoming a practicing lawyer. With his father's business acumen, Alex and his partners run a venture capital firm in Houston. Both boys share their father's passion for sports, especially soccer, tennis, fishing, and the NY Yankees.

The sudden absence of Gordon's seemingly boundless energy and intellect left his investment banker coworkers in shock. They began trading "Gordo" stories. Many involved Gordon's interactions with coworkers, clients, and support staff. Gordon asked about family members, made bets, traded jokes and sports trivia with nearly everyone. To honor his life, his coworkers established a college scholarship fund for the offspring of financial services industry staff.

The Gordon A. Rich Memorial Foundation was established in 2001. Gordon's coworkers, family, and friends continue to raise funds and devote their time and energy to help worthy young people attend college. During its first twenty-five years, this foundation provided nearly $5 million in college scholarships to more than 140 bright, hard-working students who needed financial help. As the original GAR Board and Committee members are aging, we are passing the torch to the next generation. Gordon's sons are now running this scholarship foundation, as are many of the early GAR scholar graduates. More information can be found at gordonrich.org.

Although we continue to miss Gordon, we appreciate that he is remembered in such a meaningful way.

16

Ain't Finished Yet!

I am in the fight of my life! Yes! I have been in many fights. I fought against segregated public facilities. I fought laws that humiliate Brown and Black people. I fought efforts to discriminate against women. This fight, however, is different. Many millions have coalesced into an army of seniors. People with disabilities, first defenders who risked and often gave their lives to protect their fellow man, and countless others have joined my army.

We're fighting soaring health care costs in the insurance, pharmaceutical, and hospital industries. The United States spends more on health care than any other industrial nation and has the worst. Those behind outrageous increases represent money and greed, while we champion right and justice.

At ninety-two, I am constantly seeking new recruits to make it clear to Wall Street financiers, hedge fund operators, ultra-wealthy shareholders, private equity firms, crypto traders, and venture capitalists that this is our city. We built it, and our country as well. We will not let them treat us like serfs, undermine our will, and destroy our ever-present commitment to a better life for ourselves, our children, and our children's children. For me, this means my grandchildren and great-grandchildren—Max and Ellen, Alex, Issac and Louis—and my beloved daughter-in-law, MaryAnn.

Former Secretary of Education William Bennett defined our army: "G. K. Chesterton observed that 'the true soldier fights not because he hates what is in front of him, but because he loves what is behind [or next to] him.' We fight not for hatred of our enemies but love of our fellow soldiers and the ideals of our country."

Always in the background, health care became a prominent concern when my husband, Marvin, became ill with Parkinson's and dementia. We were married for sixty-two years. He was White and I am Black. But these were physical differences. On the inside we were truly one—joined in a struggle to make the world a lot better than we found it. I was rarely sick and neither was Marvin. Fortunately, he was included in my NYC Board of Education health care plan and then in my CUNY employee Medicare plan. He retired, but I continued to work. Accompanying me daily to my office, Marvie immersed himself in books. But soon, he could no longer find his way home, much less around the city. When we left the subway, he couldn't recall common destinations. He often stumbled at home or on the street. Marvie passed away in December 2019.

When I first became a teacher in 1962, New York City promised all employees premium-free traditional Medicare upon retirement. We agreed to a smaller salary in return, which New York City is now trying to deny us. Medical bills from Marvie's various doctors in 2019 appeared reasonable and were all covered by my NYC plan. Current and future NYC retirees will not receive the same benefits.

Marvie was the president of the local chapter of Americans for Democratic Action (NYCADA) for many years. I was executive director. This chapter also hosted the annual National ADA Roosevelt Day Dinner, which attracted both national and local labor leaders from all over the country. But when Marvie began to decline, we couldn't hold regular meetings. Our NYCADA chapter membership was also declining. Many were aging—like Marvie and me—and no longer had the energy to prepare or testify before various local and state committees on specific topics like health care, funding for public transportation, etc.

The retiree chapter of my union—the Professional Staff Congress (PSC)—represents City University of New York (CUNY) faculty. I am a professional activist. As a member of the Defend the Social Safety Net Committee of the PSC, I spearheaded new activities—hosting speakers from the Economic Policy Institute; publishing a pamphlet defending the safety net; and creating an exhibit on Labor Arts (www.laborarts.org), which celebrates the labor movement and working people. Among the campuses I visited was Hostos Community College in the Bronx. Faculty member and chapter chair Lizette Colon became my partner in crime when we took the struggle to defend traditional Medicare and the broader safety net citywide.

Nevertheless, I became frustrated with the committee's limited reach when, in 2021, then-mayor Eric Adams tried to remove 250,000 municipal retirees from the premium-free, traditional Medicare plan the city promised into perpetuity. They wanted to transfer retirees into a profit-making, private Medicare Advantage plan operated by Aetna, a division of CVS.

This was the beginning of a campaign led by remarkable seniors with a spectacular woman at the helm. Marianne Pizzitola, a retired Fire Department EMT, sustained injuries in the infamous 9/11 attack in New York City's financial district. As leader of the New York

Conference of Mayors (NYCOMR), Pizzitola hired a law firm and sued the city on behalf of the 250,000 retirees the mayor's proposed action would harm. I traveled with her to Washington, DC, and to Albany, NY, to lobby state and federal officials.

Her story—our story—is that Medicare Advantage (MA) is poor health care. Unlike traditional health care, networks are limited, doctors are numerically insufficient, and reliance on prior approval is unacceptable. Those captured by Medicare Advantage plans know they delay and deny care, often putting patient lives in jeopardy. Shady techniques to make even more money are best illustrated by "upcoding," where the patient is certified to have more health issues than he/she does and the provider gets paid even more money.

Poor, working-class, and middle-class people suffer as powerful groups prosper at our expense. New York Assembly and Senate bills retaining our coverage languish as millions of retirees and others live in the shadows of poor health care. These bodies refuse to act. At the federal level, restorative bills face strong opposition from a bevy of opponents, including municipal unions. Many municipal retirees collecting traditional Medicare worked in low-level jobs and have very small pensions. A forced transfer to MA would hurt them significantly by limiting their access to quality health care. AARP—which has received billions of dollars from the United Health Group—leads the effort to enroll MA patients.

Codifying our state and federal health care rights has been the challenge of my life since 2019. It is too often said that one person can't make a difference. Don't believe it. We are an army of ones, and we're all making a difference. Recognizing the power and flexibility of nonviolent direct action I learned from Marvin, I march, parade, picket, and rally citywide. I speak at a host of events and use every opportunity to tell our story. I approach, fight, resist, and attack the issue with energy, enthusiasm, intelligence, and vision.

For decades, unions negotiated health care benefits for state and federal retirees. The older, mostly male dominated union leadership fiercely resisted and continues to resist efforts to remove health care coverage from their grasp. A large group of organizations and individuals has emerged to counter their opposition. Metro NY Health Care for All and Physicians for a National Health Program lead the pack.

Be A Hero exposes the limits of health care for patients with ALS and other diseases. Ain't I a Woman leads the fight for elderly—primarily minority—home attendants whose health and lives are endangered as they care for even more elderly poor recipients of Medicaid. The Cross Union Retirees Organizing Committee

(CROC)—small but effective—has deservedly grown in influence and credibility using varied techniques and will power. *Work-Bites*, an electronic newspaper, supports our struggle. Small, independent newspapers help, including *Gotham Gazette*, *City & State*, and *The City*.

We used the judicial system to delay the implementation of a Medicare Advantage plan. The rollout was slipshod and failed to give people enough information to decide if they wanted the plan. The court delayed the implementation, and one vendor dropped out. The city was then forced to re-negotiate the plan, and we used the courts again. We sued, and the insurance company's lawyers admitted that people would die due to the denial of care required by prior authorizations.

We had such an immense turnout that a larger courtroom of the New York County Supreme Court was used. We won that case, but the city appealed to the Appellate Division. When we won there, the city appealed to the Court of Appeals. I was part of a large contingent that took a bus to Albany. Our presence delivered a powerful message, and was remarked upon by the press. Otherwise, we won all of our lawsuits, but for the case we won by losing.

The New York Supreme Court, the trial court, agreed that the city promised us premium-free health care upon retirement. The Court of Appeals, however, agreed with the mayor that we had not proven our case about a promise. But we made several other arguments in our initial lawsuit, and the trial court only decided the promise issue. The Court of Appeals sent the case back to the trial court to decide other arguments we raised. Consequently, this lawsuit is still active, and politics intervened. Seeking re-election in 2025, Mayor Adams lost critical support over his refusal to support traditional Medicare promises, and his use of taxpayer funds to fight our court victories. During his campaign, he promised that he would not force us into an Advantage Plan. In effect, we won this part of the case after losing in the NY Court of Appeals. (Adams dropped out of the campaign on September 28, 2025.)

Our education efforts also encouraged Medicare Advantage recipients who are not within our ranks to join our demands for quality care. A result: Aetna, the CVS dispenser of Medicare Advantage, lost several billion dollars in 2024. Shareholders were unhappy, but advocates of quality traditional Medicare were ecstatic.

Grabbing the attention of state and federal officials, our NYC fight spilled into other arenas. I tell my audiences that we will ultimately win because there are more of us than there are of them. We will dismantle and ultimately expose their arguments, along with the nefarious goals of their supporters. We will never give up because right and justice will prevail. One in every five New Yorkers (1.8 million) is over sixty years of age. At sixty-five, they are eligible for Medicare. Twenty-nine percent of seniors live below the poverty line and/or are challenged by disabilities and/or isolation.

* * *

My activism began, as noted, when I was a senior at Bryn Mawr College in 1954. Along with Marvie, I helped support the Freedom Rides of the 1960s through CORE. I often remind audiences that the sit-ins and Freedom Rides transformed the nation with four lasting effects:

1) They resulted in enforcement of the Interstate Commerce Commission's ban on segregation and discrimination of public facilities; 2) They served as a forerunner of the ensuing women's movement; and 3–4) They influenced passage of both the Voting Rights Act and Medicare in 1965. What a legacy led primarily by young people at great personal sacrifice.

And now, ironically, my final major battle is centered on the very program our efforts helped inspire: Medicare. I tell audiences about my husband, Marvin's, dominant role in the Congress of Racial Equality (CORE) and his close associates in the civil rights movement—Martin

Luther King, James Farmer, Bayard Rustin, Whitney Young, and Roy Wilkins. I reveal their private discussions with then-president John F. Kennedy and his brother, Attorney General Robert F. Kennedy.

I share President Kennedy's assertion to this small group that if they wanted change, they must press him to initiate that change. Kennedy urged Marvin and the others to continue their direct-action techniques—sit-ins, freedom rides, picketing, and more—in order to publicly pressure him and his brother, the attorney general, to act. He emphasized the powerful opposition, telling Marvin and the rest of the group that his future actions on behalf of minorities were in their hands, not his. Powerful change did follow. And I'm still heeding his words.

But my story does not end here. I am also active in my community, and especially in my own building, where I organized new ways to increase our quality of life. Aging does not mean waiting to die. It means building a new life in new ways. Our programs are refreshing, imaginative, very much needed and appreciated. For example, I initiated a "buddy system" for the five hundred units in our building. It simply entails speaking with your "buddy" once a day to combat loneliness. Several other buildings in our complex asked for my help in creating a buddy system.

We know that loneliness and isolation too often result in heart disease, diabetes, stroke, and depression. I'm doing everything in my power to combat this epidemic. I also organized card games, concerts, and lectures. We celebrate the Super Bowl, Kentucky Derby, US Open, and of course Christmas and Hanukkah. When COVID stopped us, we held potluck meals in our lovely garden. These events affirmed life!

My good trouble fight continues. I'm not finished yet.

Acknowledgments

My appreciation to Skyhorse president Tony Lyons for shining a light on my decades of service, and for his confidence that a woman in her nineties has important stories to share.

Special thanks to New York literary agent Karen Gantz for convincing me to write the book, believing I could achieve it, and for recommending Dr. Joyce Starr as my personal editor and book coach. Joyce perfected each chapter, while inspiring new chapters and fresh perspectives on my material. Retaining my voice throughout—which meant so much to me—she helped me honor people and memories I hold dear with utmost sensitivity.

To my loving and supportive daughter-in-law, MaryAnn, thank you from the depths of my heart and spirit.